Enlargement and the Future of Europe

Michael Kaeding • Johannes Pollak •
Paul Schmidt
Editors

Enlargement and the Future of Europe

Views from the Capitals

Editors
Michael Kaeding
University of Duisburg-Essen
Duisburg, Germany

Johannes Pollak
Webster Vienna Private University
Vienna, Austria

Paul Schmidt
Austrian Society for European Politics
Vienna, Austria

European Commission CERV-2022-OG-SGA

ISBN 978-3-031-43233-0   ISBN 978-3-031-43234-7   (eBook)
https://doi.org/10.1007/978-3-031-43234-7

© The Editor(s) (if applicable) and The Author(s), under exclusive license to Springer Nature Switzerland AG 2023

This work is subject to copyright. All rights are solely and exclusively licensed by the Publisher, whether the whole or part of the material is concerned, specifically the rights of translation, reprinting, reuse of illustrations, recitation, broadcasting, reproduction on microfilms or in any other physical way, and transmission or information storage and retrieval, electronic adaptation, computer software, or by similar or dissimilar methodology now known or hereafter developed.

The use of general descriptive names, registered names, trademarks, service marks, etc. in this publication does not imply, even in the absence of a specific statement, that such names are exempt from the relevant protective laws and regulations and therefore free for general use.

The publisher, the authors, and the editors are safe to assume that the advice and information in this book are believed to be true and accurate at the date of publication. Neither the publisher nor the authors or the editors give a warranty, expressed or implied, with respect to the material contained herein or for any errors or omissions that may have been made. The publisher remains neutral with regard to jurisdictional claims in published maps and institutional affiliations.

This Springer imprint is published by the registered company Springer Nature Switzerland AG
The registered company address is: Gewerbestrasse 11, 6330 Cham, Switzerland

Paper in this product is recyclable.

The European Commission's support for the production of this publication does not constitute an endorsement of the contents, which reflect the views only of the authors, and the Commission cannot be held responsible for any use which may be made of the information contained herein

Foreword

These are certainly not times of 'business as usual'. The stark geopolitical reality at Europe's borders has been harshly underlined by the unjustified Russian war of aggression against Ukraine. This conflict serves as a grim reminder that the stakes are incredibly high and hence the enlargement paths we tread become more crucial than ever before.

Finding ourselves at the precipice of escalating tensions fomented by Russia not only on Ukraine, but also on nations such as Moldova and Georgia, we are called upon to bolster our partnerships, forging a lattice of interconnectivity. However, creating closer bonds with these countries is not about altruism, but rather collective resilience and a shared future for the entire continent based on peace, stability, security and economic growth.

By strengthening the ties that bind our civil societies, the beating heart of our democracies, we can catalyse transformative change. It is our commitment to empower these nations, bolstering their fight for freedom, democratic ideals and integration. By aiding their transition within a framework of the enlargement process, we aim to ensure that they elevate their socio-economic and democratic infrastructures to meet EU standards, anchored in the bedrock of the Single Market, the Green Deal and the European Pillar of Social Rights.

However, this enlargement question comes with a suite of existential interrogations, brilliantly laid out in this book. Each accession to the EU made our Union grow not only in population, but also in diversity. Accordingly, now more than ever it is of paramount importance to reflect on the aspirations, apprehensions and appraisals that fuel debate on the future of EU enlargement. These range from hopes for enhanced economic prosperity and regional stability to concerns about national sovereignty as well as the cultural and political coherence of an expanded Union.

For this purpose, we need to encourage a respectful, informed dialogue, emphasising the importance of understanding and acknowledging the diverse national perspectives that enrich our collective European identity. The EU's strength lies not only in its diversity, but also the unity that emerges from it. We have all certainly benefited from our Member States' disparate and specific experiences in the past enlargements. Economic factors, historical experiences, geopolitical considerations and cultural identities shape individual countries' stances and of course complexify the enlargement equation, but the past year has also shown how united all Member States can be in supporting a country fighting for its European path. EU citizens certainly continue to exhibit this unwavering solidarity with Ukraine, as demonstrated by the February 2023 Eurobarometer findings, with active support for: humanitarian aid (91%); welcoming displaced individuals (88%); financial assistance (77%); imposing sanctions (74%); banning Russian state-owned media (67%); and funding military equipment (65%).

It is truly inspiring to witness the enthusiasm and strong European identity displayed by countries looking for EU accession. One simply has to walk in the streets of Kyiv, Chișinău and Tbilisi to witness the remarkable display of EU flags adorning their streets and public buildings. This serves as a powerful reminder that the desire for European integration is still more relevant than ever. Such fervour should serve as a motivation for current EU members, reaffirming the importance and potential of the European Union as a force for positive change and progress.

The civil societies, ranging from social partners (trade unions and employers) to various sectors and interests, including environmental protection, human rights, social justice and economic development, are often the most European components of these countries. Hence, we not only have to nurture the capacity of these organisations at national level, promoting regional cooperation and facilitating the exchange of expertise, but we should also go one step further. We must involve the civil societies of these countries fighting for joining the EU in shaping the house they aim to be part of by encouraging their participation in the EU's decision-making process.

Far from being merely a symbolic gesture, this will foster a deeper understanding of our Union and facilitate their future integration. By taking part in this process, each civil society organisation will gain first-hand insights into the complexity of the EU decision-making process, challenges faced and factors which must be considered. It will allow them to grasp the intricacies of European governance, institutions and procedures. However, we also have a lot to hear from them and we can tap into a wealth of valuable insights and alternative viewpoints to enrich the quality of our reflection. Finally, history and policy network theory have shown that integration is also a matter of people becoming used to working with each other. Drawing closer together civil servants, civil societies and society at large will be key in cementing mutual understanding.

To conclude, as we step into the future, we must remember that the European project's essence lies in its ability to adapt, evolve and grow. We must keep alive the spirit of unity in diversity that has sustained Europe through its history and is in its DNA. EU enlargement is more than a geopolitical strategy; it is an embodiment of the European ideal of inclusive progress and shared prosperity, an ideal which is sometimes best perceived by looking at our Union from the outside.

European Economic and Social Committee   Oliver Röpke
Brussels, Belgium

Keywords

EU enlargement policies, Future of Europe, European integration, Public perception of the EU enlargement process

Why This Book?

Enhancing the European Union's (EU) resilience and that of its neighbourhood is crucial during times of great global, regional and national uncertainties, emanating from mounting security challenges such as geopolitical rivalry, military threats and the erosion of democratic values. The EU's most prominent and promising tools for engagement in the East and Western Balkans are its enlargement and neighbourhood policies. Consequently, any debate on the Union's future must include not only detailed discussion, but also decisive action regarding its reforming and extending European integration.

Russia's war of aggression in Ukraine has fundamentally changed the EU enlargement policy's context and the Union's functioning, essentially by bringing about a return of geopolitics. Employing various means ranging from economic and political influence to disinformation, electoral interferences, cyber-attacks and even military violence, Russia's exercise of neo-imperial control in the former Soviet Union states puts all countries on high alert and in positions of great vulnerability, which affects especially those in the EU's Eastern neighbourhood and Western Balkans, not only by calling into question the fundamental principles of a rules-based international order, but also challenging EU values and interests. Their dependencies on geopolitical powers such as China, Russia, Türkiye and the West are put under serious scrutiny. A choice must be made. The EU still puts considerable emphasis on conditionality, but will likely have to move away from an enlargement policy focusing overwhelmingly on incremental reform to an alternative which is about the future of democracy and the political survival of independent, self-determining states.

Meanwhile, Ukraine and Moldova were granted EU candidate status in June 2022, whilst Bosnia and Herzegovina's application received the green light in December 2022. Hence, they joined the group of official EU candidate countries, which also includes Türkiye (since 1999), North Macedonia (since 2005), Montenegro (since 2010), Serbia (since 2012) and Albania (since 2014). Georgia and Kosovo applied for EU membership in 2022 and are so far considered potential candidate countries. However, the EU is visibly struggling to respond, having been absorbed by other crises and the war's impact.

The EU's enlargement and neighbourhood strategy requires new political answers, despite the former for a long time having been regarded as one of the EU's most successful foreign policy instruments. After successive waves of EU enlargement (Denmark, Ireland and the United Kingdom in 1973; Greece in 1981; Portugal and Spain in 1986; Austria, Finland and Sweden in 1995; Cyprus, Czech Republic, Estonia, Hungary, Latvia, Lithuania, Malta, Poland, Slovakia and Slovenia in 2004; Bulgaria and Romania in 2007; and Croatia in 2013), the unquestionably positive overall assessment of enlargement has given way to public scepticism over the last decade, which varies considerably across EU countries. The so-called enlargement fatigue has become a critical issue in the internal deliberations of EU institutions, Member States and especially public opinion present dynamics and momentum which have yet to be seized and controlled. However, the criteria are clear and the Union knows no fast-track procedure or shortcuts to the enlargement process. At the same time, it is still striving to absorb and digest previous decades' enlargement rounds and the United Kingdom's EU exit.

Enlargement certainly has the potential to contribute to EU resilience-building. The 2020 review of this process strengthened the EU's conditionality by emphasising fundamentals and introducing the principle of reversibility. However, the EU's prioritisation of stability and peace-building at the expense of democracy promotion coupled with unfavourable domestic conditions in candidate countries suggests that so far it has failed to deliver on its promises. Hence, now more than ever re-thinking enlargement and neighbourhood policies for a resilient Europe is vital for the EU's future.

Here, a credible conditional membership perspective is key. Enlargement has always been considered as one of the EU's most successful foreign policy instruments to promote democracy because membership signifies credibility, which is borne out by strong academic evidence: 'Trade, partnership and cooperation agreements do not have that effect alone; association is only effective if it comes with an explicit membership perspective'.

But is the Union ready for enlargement? Or could new rounds on the horizon trigger EU reforms? This issue is inextricably linked to the debate on internal institutional functioning and 'deepening' of EU integration. Even without further enlargement, an increasing number of Member States have raised concerns about the EU's capability to act, not only with regard to decision-making procedures and national veto rights in the Council, but also bearing in mind the European Commission's sheer size. Other countries feared that the centre of political gravity would, after 2004 and 2007, move even further to the East, thereby potentially weakening their ability to define the Europe of tomorrow. Consequently, the Council's latest conclusions on enlargement approved on 14 December 2021 stress the need 'for fair and rigorous conditionality and the principle of own merits' as well as 'the importance of ensuring that the EU can maintain and deepen its own development, including its capacity to integrate new Members'. The Council further stated that its revised enlargement methodology, with an even stronger focus on fundamental reforms, aims to reinvigorate the accession process by making it 'more predictable, more credible, more dynamic, and subject to stronger political steering, based on objective criteria and rigorous positive and negative conditionality, and reversibility'. Hence, questions to do with frontloading certain accession process benefits and making the enlargement path more beneficial for people on the ground are on the agenda.

Since the EU's enlargement policy is a geostrategic investment not only in peace and stability, but also security and economic growth, as a political priority it must now be adapted to the new situation in which military aggression and political exploitation of economic and political dependencies are once again being used as foreign policy tools in Europe. Hence, in light of Russia's war in Ukraine, the European Council's strategic discussion of 23–24 June 2022 on EU relations with its partners in Europe also discussed proposals to launch a European political community in order 'to offer a platform for political coordination for European countries across the continent'. This European political community could foster political dialogue and cooperation among all European countries with whom the EU has close relations, by providing opportunities to address issues of common interest, such as energy, security, climate and economic relations, thereby strengthening the security, stability and prosperity of the European continent, its strategic alliances and geopolitical sphere of influence. However, it is explicitly not intended to replace the existing EU enlargement procedures, which would for the time being continue to be based on established criteria. Nevertheless, other options might also be on the table, such as: a renewed European Free Trade Association; joining the European Economic Area; different degrees of membership; a staged accession process or a combination of various options.

All countries face unique and exceptional circumstances to which EU decision-making must adapt. Thinking 'outside of the box' and helping to improve people's understanding of these issues might be a cumbersome exercise, yet it is important not to focus on limitations, but rather on new possibilities, best practices and joint solutions. Furthermore, in view of its transformative power, does the EU want to play a similar role for Ukraine and other candidate countries that it played between the 1970s until 10 years ago by helping candidates and new members transition into full-fledged democracies?

To understand commonalities and differences across Europe, this volume offers national views from the 27 EU Member States and 14 selected countries in the EU's vicinity, analysing in short and concise chapters a variety of aspects concerning their respective forward-looking visions regarding the EU's political agenda for the Eastern Neighbourhood and Western Balkans.

When talking about EU enlargement, you will notice that geography matters a great deal. Until the start of Russia's war of aggression in Ukraine, for most countries the key focus was primarily on the Western Balkan countries due to their proximity. Indeed, for various reasons certain countries have attached strategic importance to this region.

Austria, for example, is home to 600,000 people with roots in the Balkans. With Austrian companies, in areas such as finance, telecommunication, construction and tourism, being among the top investors in what is considered their 'home market', economic interests also go hand in hand with the rationale of supporting South-Eastern Europe. For Slovenia the Western Balkan countries comprise the second largest trading partner, generating 14% of Slovenian exports in 2022. Furthermore, it is the region where most (70%) Slovenian outward investments are directed. The largest number of foreign workers in Slovenia come from the Western Balkans, clearly reflecting historical ties that Slovene people have with other ex-Yugoslav republics. Most countries believe that adopting EU standards and values is the only way to produce long-term stability and prosperity in the Western Balkans and thus of key relevance for stability and security throughout the EU.

Conversely, Sweden and Poland represent other EU countries that have traditionally been part of the pro-EU enlargement camp to the 'East', taking, for example, the EU's 2009 Eastern Partnership initiative to provide closer support for integrating countries in the Union's Eastern Neighbourhood.

Then there are countries, including Portugal, which despite being geographically distanced on the Union's western edge, have been supporters of successive enlargement rounds as a form of solidarity and settling a 'debt of gratitude'. However, the Portuguese attitude has shifted. Although agreeing to grant Ukraine and Moldova candidate status, it was one of the last States to confirm its support publicly. Both the Western Balkans and Eastern regions are far away from a Portuguese perspective, not only geographically, but also historically, culturally and emotionally. There is absolutely no connection between Portugal and the Western Balkan countries, nor Ukraine, Moldova or Georgia. In fact, nobody talks about EU enlargement in Portugal.

Russia's war in Ukraine though has brought a tangible security-political shift towards enlargement. Over the last two decades Russia's interests in the Western Balkans region have mostly been political, based on a strategy of increasing its influence by aligning with pro-Russian sympathisers in the region's countries. This became extremely important when Russia invaded Ukraine on 24 February 2022. Shortly thereafter on 6 March as a direct consequence of the war's profound change in EU security, a referendum on abolition of the Danish defence opt-out—one of four in total—was announced by the EU. This was decided as part of a broad multi-party defence agreement reached during the invasion's first two weeks. The referendum held on 1 June 2022 gave an overwhelming 'yes' to abolition with two-thirds of the votes voting in favour. The first reaction of the Danish Prime Minister Mette Frederiksen was that this vote 'sent a clear signal to Vladimir Putin'.

With Russia's war in Ukraine, the values associated with belonging to the West have also become more important than ever. Hence, whereas previously support for enlargement was mainly motivated by economic interests, today a values-based attitude prevails.

Moreover, for many enlargement has now become a necessary geopolitical tool, with any perceived slowdown threatening to increase other actors' influence, largely Russia and China (but also Türkiye). Nevertheless, the Western Balkans remains a key area for the EU in terms of energy, migration and security. That is why, *inter alia*, Czechia has strongly supported a financial package to reduce the region's

Russian energy dependence, whilst at the same time expecting the Western Balkan States in return to share the EU's foreign policy values towards Russia. Furthermore, Denmark argues that if the EU keeps these Western Balkans countries outside for too long, they may well turn to China, Türkiye and Russia. Similarly, the Swedish minister for EU affairs has expressed a view that EU enlargement is one of the Union's best geopolitical tools and a way of creating security and stability in Europe.

However, are people generally aware of enlargement's geopolitical relevance, or are there other issues which seem to be more significant? In the spring of 2022, 57% of Belgian public opinion was in favour of enlargement, which is exactly the European average, halfway between Lithuania (81%) and Austria (33%). Strangely, Austria's position on EU accession for the Western Balkans is one of the few examples where the country does not pander to public opinion. In fact, Austria and France are unusual in being the only two countries where public perception of enlargement has long been consistently negative.

Overall, though, people in the EU do not consider that the six Western Balkan countries are ready for membership yet due to concerns related to the rule of law, corruption, organised crime and a perceived high risk of increasing immigration, should any receive full membership. This position has united both the left and right. In Denmark, for example, an opinion poll in 2018 showed that: 69% of liberal-conservative voters opposed enlargement in the Western Balkans because of ideological opposition to globalisation and fears about the dangers of immigration, whereas 53% of the left opposed enlargement because of social dumping and its risks to the Danish model as well as its welfare state.

However, a larger EU also creates questions about the workings of the Union itself. Various EU leaders have outlined ideas about moving to majority voting in issues currently requiring unanimity, for instance in parts of economic affairs and foreign policy. Following the Conference of the Future of Europe, though, 13 Member States declared that they did not support EU treaty changes. On 21 November 2022, the Portuguese Prime Minister António Costa stated that under its current institutional and budgetary framework the EU does not have sufficient capacity to meet the proposed enlargement's expectations. He even warned that false promises could produce dramatic consequences, going on to stress that while the EU has very clear criteria for the accession of new Member States, unfortunately it does not have any criteria regarding its own capacity to integrate other Members.

How then should the Union prepare and adapt for a larger political community? Sweden is in favour of using 'passerelle' clauses in the current treaty to facilitate a move to qualified majority voting in certain areas of the Common Foreign and Security Policy, but is otherwise against any further EU reforms. Regarding the EU reform agenda, Austria is currently reluctant to support the general introduction of majority voting, given the importance of veto power for smaller Member States. However, it does propose, *inter alia*: a move from unanimity to majority voting in foreign policy; a joint European seat in the United Nations Security Council; a smaller European Commission with a rotation system; formal establishment of the EU-Spitzenkandidaten process for the presidency of the European Commission; a true right of initiative; as well as a single seat for the European Parliament and the expansion of the co-decision procedure to more policy areas. Interestingly, while Austria was initially part of a group of Member States that advocated ruling out treaty changes resulting from the Conference on the Future of Europe, the current conservative-green coalition supports a new EU Treaty and has therefore signalled its wish to follow up on Conference recommendations with a Treaty Convention.

Furthermore, existing border issues need to be resolved. Ever since its 2013 accession Croatia has taken advantage of a right to veto the opening of new negotiating chapters in Serbia's and Montenegro's EU accession processes, thus reminiscent of Slovenia's behaviour towards Croatia some 15 years earlier.

Lastly, some EU countries will strongly push the rule of law discussion within the EU and stand firmly against any democratic backsliding within the Union. Some countries have underlined that new EU Member States will need to adhere to *all* the Union's rules before joining.

In order to maintain a credible enlargement process following a merit-based approach more strongly focussed on fundamental reforms, such as the rule of law, fundamental rights, a functioning economy and democratic institutions, some countries are ready to push for and accept flexibility in the enlargement process. They see a need to put aside old national resentments and for the EU to deliver on its commitments, including financial support and a clear roadmap for accelerating and deepening neighbouring partners' reforms. This means involving the candidate countries in selected policies (such as the Single Market) before full Membership is achieved. The Czech economy, for example, is heavily export-oriented, a position which may be offset by expansion of the internal market. Moreover, the post-war reconstruction of Ukraine is generally seen as a huge future opportunity.

Ultimately, many agree that the geopolitical situation in Europe impacted by Russian aggression against Ukraine offers the EU unique chances to enlarge geographically, which in turn increases the prospects for deepening integration in terms of security and defence.

Furthermore, existing Member States could serve as role models for specific applicants (as Denmark did for Estonia in its pre-accession process). For every applicant there are specific inducements that would help to convert enlargement into a key political priority. The Belgium 2024 EU Presidency could initiate an exercise on the 'cost of non-enlargement' inspired by the report on the 'cost of non-Europe' presented by Paolo Cecchini in 1988.

To sum up, our 41 short contributions certainly enhance our understanding of national differences and initial positions in establishing a common European future enlargement and neighbourhood strategy. Revealed in this way, these chapters provide a thought-provoking kaleidoscope of diverse approaches across the continent, which must be considered when developing new policies for the Union.

This volume helps by improving our appreciation of European countries with diverse levels of integration and cooperation. It analyses the different EU and European experiences as well as approaches to Europe's future enlargement and neighbourhood strategy, the way it is perceived by its people and its overall importance for the future of Europe. The book also addresses an audience far beyond the typical academic niche interested in European politics. It is rather a guidebook in our 'Views from the Capitals' series, taking us through a tremendously varying and exciting political landscape of Europe that is constantly changing. Its countries constitute the individual and unique pieces of a puzzle, which together reveal a bigger European picture.

As a guidebook, it favours lexical purpose as much as comprehensive comparative reading. Students and teachers may find scores of questions, differences and common ground to explore more deeply in seminar papers and theses. Practitioners will benefit from the short overviews being presented on possibly the biggest topical issue of our times and for all of us who are interested readers it demonstrates the breathtaking diversity that defines, divides and ultimately unites this continent.

We are particularly grateful to Eva Ribera, Project Manager at the Trans European Policy Studies Association (TEPSA), and Anna Rauchenwald, intern at the Österreichische Gesellschaft für Europapolitik (ÖGfE), for their editorial processing and tireless efforts in making this project become a reality.

June 2023

Michael Kaeding
Johannes Pollak
Paul Schmidt

Contents

Part I Member States

Enlarging and Reforming the European Union: An Austrian
Perspective... 3
Katrin Auel and Paul Schmidt

Belgium: If the Enlargement Process Is Broken, Then Fix It.......... 7
Jean-Louis De Brouwer

Bulgaria's Attitude Towards EU Enlargement........................ 11
Ivan Nachev and Hristo Panchugov

Croatia: Between Proclaimed Enthusiasm and Reality on the
Ground.. 15
Hrvoje Butković

The National Debate in Cyprus on the Future of EU Enlargement
Policy... 19
Giorgos Kentas

The Czech Approach to EU Enlargement: Full Steam Ahead!......... 23
Zdeněk Sychra and Petr Kratochvíl

Denmark's Position on Enlargement................................. 29
Zlatko Jovanovic and Marcus Popov Damgaard

Estonia: Supporting Fast-Track Enlargements....................... 33
Viljar Veebel

Finland Should Focus on EU Reforms Ahead of Enlargement........ 39
Juha Jokela

What Infuriating French Reluctance Reveals........................ 43
Christian Lequesne and Olivier Rozenberg

Strong Tailwinds for EU Enlargement in Germany: But EU
Membership Has a Price Tag.. 47
Funda Tekin

Greece, EU Enlargement and the 'Thessaloniki Promise' 51
Daniel Furby and Dimitris Tsaknis

Enlargement at All Costs? A View from Hungary 55
Veronika Czina, Tamás Szigetvári, and Gábor Túry

Further Enlargement of the European Union: The View from Dublin .. 61
John O'Brennan

Beyond 'Enlargement Fatigue': A View from Rome 65
Matteo Bonomi

Head and Heart in the Right Place: Latvia on the EU Enlargement 71
Aleksandra Palkova and Karlis Bukovskis

**Lithuania's Strong Support for the EU's 'Open Door' Policy: How
to Make Use of the Geopolitical Window of Opportunity** 75
Ramūnas Vilpišauskas

Luxembourg: Get Ready to Enlarge 79
Guido Lessing

Malta and Enlargement: Supportive But Not Engaged 83
Mark Harwood

Direction East: Polish Views on the EU's Enlargement Policy 87
Natasza Styczyńska

Portugal: Nobody Talks About Enlargement 91
Alice Cunha

**Romania's Constant Support for the Enlargement Process: A
Proof of Investment in European Values** 95
Mihai Sebe and Eliza Vaș

**Slovakia's Approach to EU Enlargement: From Strategic Passivity
and Declaratory Supporter into the Reformist Vanguard** 99
Matej Navrátil and Lucia Mokrá

Slovenia: A Strong Defender of Western Balkan Enlargement 103
Maja Bučar and Boštjan Udovič

**Spain: From a Reluctant Supporter to a True Defendant of
Enlargement?** 107
Raquel García Llorente and Ignacio Molina

**Sweden and EU Enlargement: A Strong Supporter Walking a Fine
Line** 111
Calle Håkansson

Strict, Fair, Engaged.... And Still Without a Vision? A View from
the Netherlands on EU Enlargement and Its Neighbourhood 115
Giselle Bosse

Part II   EU Neighbours

What Is Holding Back Albania? 123
Tanushe Muhametaj

Between Hopes and Frustrations: Bosnia's Path to the EU Is No Shorter
Despite EU Candidacy Status 127
Vedran Dzihic

Seizing the EU Enlargement Momentum: Georgia's Prospects for
Joining the European Family 131
Irakli Sirbiladze, Mariam Khotenashvili, and Elene Panchulidze

Iceland's Passive Supportive Approach: Vocal with Others
on Ukraine 135
Baldur Thorhallsson

Kosovo's Leap of Faith for EU Membership 139
Naim Rashiti

How Should the EU Support Moldova's Path Towards Accession? 145
Iulian Groza and Mihai Mogildea

The Scramble for Enlargement: Montenegro 149
Danijela Jacimovic and Zorica Kalezic

North Macedonia: Stuck on the EU's Doorstep? 153
Irena Rajchinovska Pandeva

Norway: A Non-member But Active Supporter of EU Enlargement 157
Pernille Rieker

Serbia on a Rocky Road to the EU 161
Milena Mihajlovic

Switzerland: Not a Candidate But a Partner in EU Enlargement 165
Frank Schimmelfennig

Schrödinger's Candidate: Türkiye's Awkward Situation Within the
Enlargement Debate 169
Özgehan Şenyuva and Ali Baydarol

On the Outside Looking in: The United Kingdom After Brexit 175
Brendan Donnelly

EU Enlargement Considering New Realities: The Ukrainian
Direction 179
Yuriy Yakymenko and Mykhailo Pashkov

Contributors

Katrin Auel Institute for Advanced Studies, Vienna, Austria

Ali Baydarol Sabancı University, Tuzla, Türkiye

Matteo Bonomi Istituto Affari Internazionali, Rome, Italy

Giselle Bosse University of Maastricht, Maastricht, The Netherlands

Maja Bučar Faculty of Social Sciences, University of Ljubljana, Ljubljana, Slovenia

Karlis Bukovskis Latvian Institute of International Affairs, Riga, Latvia

Hrvoje Butković The Institute for Development and International Relations, Zagreb, Croatia

Alice Cunha Portuguese Institute of International Relations, Lisbon, Portugal

Veronika Czina Institute of World Economics, Budapest, Hungary

Marcus Popov Damgaard Democracy in Europe, Copenhagen, Denmark

Jean-Louis De Brouwer Egmont—The Royal Institute for International Relations, Brussels, Belgium

Brendan Donnelly The Federal Trust, London, UK

Vedran Dzihic Austrian Institute for International Affairs, Wien, Austria

Daniel Furby European Public Law Organization, Athens, Greece

Raquel García Llorente Elcano Royal Institute, Madrid, Spain

Iulian Groza Institute for European Policies and Reforms, Chișinău, Republic of Moldova

Calle Håkansson Swedish Institute of International Affairs, Stockholm, Sweden

Mark Harwood Institute of European Studies, University of Malta, Msida, Malta

Danijela Jacimovic Faculty of Economics of University of Montenegro, Podgorica, Montenegro

Juha Jokela Finnish Institute of International Affairs, Helsinki, Finland

Zlatko Jovanovic Democracy in Europe, Copenhagen, Denmark

Zorica Kalezic Central Bank of Montenegro, Podgorica, Montenegro

Giorgos Kentas Nicosia, Cyprus

Mariam Khotenashvili Trans European Policy Studies Association, Brussels, Belgium

Petr Kratochvíl Institute of International Relations Prague, Prague, Czechia

Milena Mihajlovic European Policy Centre, Belgrade, Serbia

Christian Lequesne Sciences Po, Paris, France

Guido Lessing Luxembourg, Esch-sur-Alzette, Luxembourg

Mihai Mogildea Institute for European Policies and Reforms, Republic of Moldova

Lucia Mokrá Comenius University Bratislava, Bratislava, Slovakia

Ignacio Molina Elcano Royal Institute, Madrid, Spain

Tanushe Muhametaj Cooperation and Development Institute, Tirana, Albania

Ivan Nachev New Bulgarian University, Sofia, Bulgaria

Matej Navrátil Comenius University Bratislava, Bratislava, Slovakia

John O'Brennan Maynooth University, Kildare, Ireland

Aleksandra Palkova Latvian Institute of International Affairs, Riga, Latvia

Elene Panchulidze PMC Research Centre, Tbilisi, Georgia

Hristo Panchusgov New Bulgarian University, Sofia, Bulgaria

Mykhailo Pashkov Razumkov Centre, Kyiv, Ukraine

Irena Rajchinovska Pandeva Faculty of Law Iustinianus Primus, Skopje, North Macedonia

Naim Rashiti Balkan Policy Research Group, Prishtina, Kosovo

Pernille Rieker Norwegian Institute of International Affairs, Oslo, Norway

Olivier Rozenberg Centre for European Studies and Comparative Politics, Sciences Po, Paris, France

Frank Schimmelfennig ETH Zurich, Zurich, Switzerland

Paul Schmidt Austrian Society for European Politics, Vienna, Austria

Mihai Sebe European Institute of Romania, Bucharest, Romania

Özgehan Şenyuva Middle East Technical University, Türkiye

Irakli Sirbiladze PMC Research Centre, Tbilisi, Georgia

Natasza Styczyńska Jagellonian University, Kraków, Poland

Zdeněk Sychra University of West Bohemia, Plzeň, Czechia

Tamás Szigetvári Institute of World Economics, Centre for Economics and Regional Studies, Budapest, Hungary

Funda Tekin Institute for European Politics, Berlin, Germany

Baldur Thorhallsson Institute of International Affairs, University of Iceland, Reykjavík, Iceland

Dimitris Tsaknis European Public Law Organization, Athens, Greece

Gábor Túry Institute of World Economics, Centre for Economics and Regional Studies, Budapest, Hungary

Boštjan Udovič Faculty of Social Sciences, University of Ljubljana, Ljubljana, Slovenia

Eliza Vaş European Institute of Romania, Bucharest, Romania

Viljar Veebel Baltic Defence College, Tartu, Estonia

Ramūnas Vilpišauskas Institute of International Relations and Political Science, Vilnius University, Vilnius, Lithuania

Yuriy Yakymenko Razumkov Centre, Kyiv, Ukraine

Part I
Member States

Enlarging and Reforming the European Union: An Austrian Perspective

Katrin Auel and Paul Schmidt

Regarding further enlargement of the European Union (EU), Austria's political priorities are beyond doubt. Ever since joining the EU in 1995, different waves of enlargement have been high on the country's agenda and this is especially true for the accession of countries in the Western Balkans. Regardless of the respective government's coalition composition, the Western Balkans' European future has been and continues to be a central priority. At the same time, there is a sense of reluctance towards starting accession negotiations with Ukraine and Moldova, not to mention a firm rejection of even considering any further talks with Türkiye.

Political Support for the European Path of the Western Balkans

Some of the main elements for this backing include the historical, geographical and cultural proximity. Today, close to 600,000 people with Balkan roots live in Austria. Moreover, Austrian companies, in areas such as finance, telecommunications, construction and tourism are among the top investors in what is considered their 'home market', with economic interests also going hand in hand with the rationale of supporting South-Eastern Europe. Its economic and social development is seen as a precondition for stability in the Western Balkans, where political vulnerabilities remain a constant challenge and threat.

One central aspect is related to security interests, such as the fight against organised crime and control of migration routes. The Western Balkans route's porousness for migrants had, for example, been one of the arguments for Austria's

---

K. Auel
Institute for Advanced Studies, Vienna, Austria
e-mail: auel@ihs.ac.at

P. Schmidt (✉)
Austrian Society for European Politics, Vienna, Austria
e-mail: paul.schmidt@oegfe.at

veto against accession to the Schengen Area for Romania and Bulgaria at the end of 2022. The EU enlargement process and critical reforms, albeit a moving target, are also seen as a crucial stabilising and security factor beyond the Western Balkans region, which is surrounded by EU countries. The Russian war against Ukraine, with its geopolitical power shift reaching the six Western Balkans countries' fragile democracies, has given further impetus to this argument and has opened new opportunities to advance with reforms and enlargement, processes often considered frustratingly slow.

The EU's green light for accession negotiations with Northern Macedonia and Albania or Austria's active lobbying for Bosnia and Herzegovina's candidate status are but some of the latest results of these priorities and provide evidence of its interest in South-Eastern Europe. However, more is needed to resolve the impasse created by enlargement negotiations and move on to support efficient democratisation of the respective countries. The Austrian government has proposed a gradual integration approach, front-loading some of the more tangible benefits to the EU candidate countries and their people. Progressive cooperation would include, for instance: phased integration into the EU Single Market; early participation in EU energy- and climate policies; EU educational programmes as well as common foreign, security and defence policies along with a crisis management mechanism.

Government vs. Public Opinion

EU accession for the Western Balkans is also one of the few examples where Austrian politics does not pander to public opinion, but takes a very different policy stance. Although public support for future enlargement has increased, especially since the Russian invasion of Ukraine, it is still one of the lowest in the EU, with only 37% in favour and 54% against further enlargement, according to the most recent Eurobarometer. In fact, Austria and France are the only two countries where public perception of enlargement has long been consistently negative. It is simply not considered to be one of the most pressing issues and hence has become openly rejected by the vast majority of people. Rather, reform and consolidation of the Union's structures and policies are seen as prerequisites for even considering the entry of new Members. Improving the cooperation between existing EU Member States is much more important to the general public, a position which has not substantially changed over the last decade.

As a result, it would seem, on the one hand, that Austrian politics has a need to explain itself. Yet, on the other hand, the government would argue that there is no trade-off because EU enlargement is seen as a medium-term process that will necessarily have to go hand in hand with reforming the Union. Regarding the EU reform-agenda, the current Austrian government is reluctant to support the general introduction of majority voting, given the importance of veto power for smaller Member States. However, it does propose *inter-alia*: a move from unanimity to majority voting in foreign policy; a joint European seat in the United Nations Security Council; a smaller European Commission with a rotation system; formal establishment of the EU-Spitzenkandidaten (leading candidates) process for the presidency of the European Commission; a true right of initiative as well as a single seat for the European Parliament and the expansion of the co-decision procedure to more policy areas. The long-standing demands of Austrian governments also include more subsidiarity and less bureaucracy, meaning, for example, a reduction of European regulation and the inclusion of expiration dates for new legislation. While Austria was initially part of a Member States group that advocated ruling out treaty changes resulting from the Conference on the Future of Europe, the current conservative-green coalition supports a new EU Treaty and claims that it would want to follow up on Conference recommendations with a Treaty Convention. However, beyond speeches and headlines, politics of support for candidate and potential candidate countries as well as a tentative list of institutional reforms, real action and tangible initiatives by the Austrian government remain scarce. Time and energy are mainly spent on solving urgent crisis-related questions rather than using leverage to move from words to European deeds.

Clearly, progress can be expected to be painstakingly slow if 27 EU Member States neither agree on enlarging the EU nor on its reform, as a potential precondition for successful enlargement. This is even more the case in a situation where the geopolitical dimension is omnipresent and managing the polycrisis with which Europe is confronted absorbs almost all available strength. Time does not seem to be ripe for institutional introspection, but for decisive crisis management, securing political will and unity. Tangible results are needed when prices are soaring and social wellbeing is under severe pressure. The ability or inability to solve the many problems at hand will also leave its impact on the legitimacy of and support for European integration. Yet, even symbolic gestures may open new horizons without having to enter the nitty-gritty complexities of national interests and long-lasting and detailed negotiations. There can be no shortcuts to EU accession, but supporting necessary reforms in the candidate countries by starting an open process with intermediate steps and merit-based assessments can in itself already be helpful. It is common knowledge that many of the EU capitals were not entirely convinced about granting candidate status to Ukraine either. It is, though, also one of those examples in the history of European integration, where EU leadership meets indecisiveness or even disregard and can thus make a remarkable difference.

Recommendations

To counter the traditionally sceptic public opinion on EU integration in general and enlargement in particular, the government should take a more proactive stance in communicating the Western Balkan region's importance, as well as Ukraine and Moldova, for the sake of Austrian and European stability in general. Far removed from topicality, Austria could engage in drafting its own medium set of priorities regarding the future of Europe based on a close consultation with civil society and interest groups including well-organised and credible feedback loops. The dialogue with its citizens should not be regarded as finished now that the Conference on the

Future of Europe has ended. Rather, a continual interchange would be crucial in raising awareness, improving understanding and securing support for strategic national priorities. With a clear set of visions, a concrete strategy and comprehensive reform proposals it could be much easier to find likeminded partners and build lasting European alliances. Once arguments are within the public domain, have gained cross-border credibility and are on the agenda for the future of Europe, a clear and convincing case can be made either for a closer partnership with the countries in the European neighbourhood or for enlarging a better functioning European Union.

Katrin Auel, Ph.D., is Head of the Research Group European Governance, Public Finance and Labour Markets at the Institute for Advanced Studies Vienna (IHS), which she joined in 2012. After completing her studies at the University of Konstanz, she held positions at the University of Halle-Wittenberg, the University of Hagen, the University of Oxford and the European University Viadrina. Her research focuses on Europeanisation and legislative studies.

IHS is an independent research institute in Austria covering the areas of Economics, Political Science and Sociology and a member of TEPSA.

Paul Schmidt has been Secretary General of the Austrian Society for European Politics since 2009. Previously he has worked at the Oesterreichische Nationalbank, both in Vienna and at their Representative Office in Brussels. He studied International Relations and Political Science at universities in Austria, Spain and USA and holds a diploma from the Diplomatic Academy of Vienna. His work mainly focuses on the analysis and discussion of medium- to long-term questions regarding European integration. Paul's comments and op-eds are regularly published in the Austrian and international media. He is a Member of the Board of TEPSA and the European Movement in Austria and co-editor of the book series 'The Future of Europe: views from the Capitals'.

The Austrian Society for European Politics was founded in 1991 and aims to promote and support information activities on European affairs in Austria and beyond. With its headquarters in Vienna, the Society is a non-governmental and non-partisan platform mainly constituted by the Austrian Social Partners and the Oesterreichische Nationalbank.

Belgium: If the Enlargement Process Is Broken, Then Fix It

Jean-Louis De Brouwer

A Belgian Zeitenwende?

In closing the last millennium, Belgium's position was reflected in a joint declaration (along with France and Italy) annexed to the Maastricht Treaty, stating that 'the strengthening of the institutions is an indispensable condition for the conclusion of the first accession negotiations'. In the spring of 1999, the country's support for enlargement was the lowest of the then 15 Member States, with only 28% of citizens in favour, compared to 63% in Sweden (the highest) and a European average of 42%.

The government was portraying accession as a global process, but one in which each application would be evaluated on a case-by-case basis according to objective criteria. It stressed that it was less a 'negotiation' than a 'discussion', with the acquis to be accepted and implemented in full. Real efforts were expected to ensure this convergence, without any deadline being set for its completion. Of course, the Union would also have to prepare itself by adapting its institutional, political and financial frameworks.

Almost a quarter of a century later, the discourse is changing. Following the outbreak of war in Ukraine, it is widely recognised that the concept of enlargement has become toxic: using the policy of enlargement, an inherently technical process of alignment, to achieve political objectives is a mistake. What is at stake is not so much preparation for the next accession, but the unification of Europe into an integrated political and economic whole. Not only is strategic interest in a stable and secure environment paramount, but the time has also come to engage in a process that is no longer one way: the Union can make offers and no longer merely express demands; it must behave more like a companion than a supervisor.

J.-L. De Brouwer (✉)
Egmont – The Royal Institute for International Relations, Brussels, Belgium
e-mail: jl.debrouwer@egmontinstitute.be

© The Author(s), under exclusive license to Springer Nature Switzerland AG 2023
M. Kaeding et al. (eds.), *Enlargement and the Future of Europe*,
https://doi.org/10.1007/978-3-031-43234-7_2

In the spring of 2022, 57% of Belgian public opinion was in favour of enlargement, which is exactly the European average (an improvement of 12% compared to the previous Eurobarometer), halfway between Lithuania (81%) and Austria (33%).

Not so Sure

On the eve of Belgium's Presidency of the European Union in the first half of 2024, this new rhetoric is remarkable. But many ambiguities remain.

The federal government keeps on evoking that strict criteria must be set and respected to which Belgium will be attentive. The need to avoid making the same mistakes of 2004 and 2007, namely accepting new Memberships when the institutions are totally unprepared, has been stressed. However, nothing precise has been put forward on what these adaptations should be, apart from the traditional reference to removing unanimity.

In short, the need may be felt to reframe the enlargement policy, to give it the flexibility it needs in responding to the geopolitical challenges of the moment and make its benefits more tangible for the populations of the countries concerned. However, there is no clear indication on the way to achieve this 'aggiornamento'.

What Is in a Concept?

In his recent book 'Diplomacy in Practice', Johan Verbeke, a seasoned Belgian diplomat and former Director General of the Egmont Institute, warns against cognitive traps and stresses that concepts tend to have a kind of intrinsic inertia. The time might have come to manipulate the enlargement concept, by changing it... or removing it altogether.

It is a truism that the present enlargement process has reached an impasse. The deepening/enlarging dilemma has not been resolved; frustrations are mounting on both sides and the recognition of the candidate status for Ukraine, Moldova and Bosnia and Herzegovina risks reinforcing this deadlock. Is it therefore not time to reflect on a new European architecture? Are we not faced this time with the challenge of a real 'Zeitenwende', a turning point, on a par with the tectonic changes that followed the Second World War and the fall of the Berlin Wall?

Milestones have been set, particularly with the Berlin Process, launched at a time when the Commission had announced a pause in the enlargement process. This was followed more recently with creation of the European Political Community (EPC), two initiatives which, it has been abundantly emphasised, should not constitute alternatives to enlargement.

Other formulae, such as the Deep and Comprehensive Free Trade Agreement with Ukraine, deserve to be explored and deepened. They would make it possible in the medium term to envisage a model which combines an extension of the internal market around a consolidated but still open Eurozone. This could be complemented by reinforced financial solidarity instruments, along the lines of the current cohesion policy. For the rest, differentiated integration modalities—whether temporary or permanent—should be accepted, pragmatically balancing the necessary coherence of internal policies and the readiness of non-Member countries to commit to them.

In this perspective, the EPC must be given attention. Holding the first meeting in October 2022 was itself a remarkable diplomatic event. However, everyone agrees that the real test will be how it evolves through the three planned meetings in 2023 and 2024. Beyond the scepticism of many, this initiative should be supported because it offers a framework where (Heads of) States can discuss as equals non-conflictual issues of common interest. On this basis, variable forms of cooperation can be envisaged, such as those identified in Prague (protection of critical infrastructure, fight against cybercrime, energy connections, higher education, mobility). Above all, it includes the candidate country systematically forgotten in all the current debates, namely Türkiye.

None of these advances will be possible if the institutional question is posed as a prerequisite. The objective must be to consolidate the continent's geopolitical stability around a development model inspired by the European Union, ensuring that the human societies concerned perceive its tangible benefits. Some will fear the complexity, or even opacity, of the institutional set-up which is likely to be generated by such an approach, but Belgium is well placed to know that good governance corresponds to the complexity of any reality to which it applies.

Recommendations

The 2004 enlargement's 20th anniversary should be an opportunity to take stock in order to draw lessons which can guide political choices that will determine the future of Europe. Belgium could certainly initiate such an exercise on the 'cost of non-enlargement', inspired by the report on the 'cost of non-Europe' presented by Paolo Cecchini in 1988.

The EPC's challenge must be taken up. Belgium can contribute to this, even if it is not foreseen in the short term as hosting a meeting of the EPC. For example, considering the institutional fluidity desired by its promoters, Belgium could act as a leader for deepening one of the selected themes, by coordinating the work of interested States.

The basic elements for defining a future European architecture are already available. However, they still need to be put together in a coherent and realistic manner, also considering the consistency of the policies stake. Here again, a Presidency at the juncture of two legislatures could play a key role. As a founding Member State, Belgium will be able to invest in this only if it accepts the consequences of these new balances with lucidity.

Jean-Louis De Brouwer is Director of the European Affairs Programme at the Egmont Institute. He joined the Institute in October 2019, after retiring from the European Commission where, as a director, he was successively in charge of immigration, asylum, visas and border policies (DG Justice and Home Affairs), implementation of the EU2020 agenda and employment policies (DG Employment, Social Affairs, and Inclusion) together with humanitarian aid operations and policies (DG European Civil Protection and Humanitarian Aid Operations).

The Egmont Institute is an independent think tank based in Brussels. Its interdisciplinary research is conducted in a spirit of total academic freedom. Drawing on the expertise of its own research fellows, as well as that of external specialists, both Belgian and foreign, it provides analysis and policy options that are meant to be as operational as possible.

Bulgaria's Attitude Towards EU Enlargement

Ivan Nachev and Hristo Panchugov

Bulgaria became part of the European Union (EU) on 1 January 2007, within the second wave of the EU's largest enlargement so far. Accordingly, as a full Member the country has been trying to follow and participate in common European policies for more than 16 years.

Following accession, Bulgarian society was engulfed with the euphoria of this enlargement process and to a large extent expected rapid improvement in the quality of life and democratisation of their political system. Unfortunately, this did not come about with the result that there has been a gradual strengthening of anti-European feelings and nationalist sentiment throughout the country. This badly affected Bulgarians' general perception of a European ideal, hence the understanding and implementation of common European policies in the country.

Many governments have contributed to this over the years by explaining the 'positives' of integration as being linked with their own good governance, whilst any crisis or problem in political governance concerned European Commission requirements for the implementation of common policies. To date, there is still a problem with the country's political representation in the EU, in that many Bulgarians remain unfamiliar with its decision-making mechanisms and question how the European institutions function. There is a lack of transparency and accountability not only for the work of Bulgarian Members of the European Parliament, but also that of ministers during their participation in the Council of the EU; mayors in the Committee of the Regions; and Bulgarian representatives in the EU's Economic and Social Committee.

Bulgaria's 16 years of EU membership has done little or nothing to improve any broad understanding of the Union. Indeed, various crises that have befallen the EU in recent years have contributed to increasing disillusionment with its policies. Although public opinion about the EU remains generally favourable (according to

---

I. Nachev · H. Panchugov (✉)
New Bulgarian University, Sofia, Bulgaria

© The Author(s), under exclusive license to Springer Nature Switzerland AG 2023
M. Kaeding et al. (eds.), *Enlargement and the Future of Europe*,
https://doi.org/10.1007/978-3-031-43234-7_3

annual surveys conducted by Alpha Research, in 2022, 56% of Bulgarians viewed the Union positively and only 13% expressed negative sentiments), there are significant drifts lurking beneath the surface. At the peak of one such trend in 2018, 65% of Bulgarians were recorded as holding positive views. However, on closer inspection 45% of Bulgarians wanted less integration and more power to Member States; 26% believed that Bulgaria had lost more than it had gained from its EU membership; 49% were convinced that Bulgaria's voice was not being taken into consideration at EU level; 66% declared that they did not have the confidence of European citizens; 50% of respondents were dissatisfied with the decisions of EU leaders; and as a result, 32% believe that parties that are against the political elite are no longer to be considered as dangerous.

Presidency of the Council of the EU

Bulgaria chaired the Council of the EU in the first half of 2018, sending messages for consensus, competitiveness and cohesion. The Presidency's motto was 'Union makes strength', coupled with a message of working hard to create a new impulse in the process of EU expansion to Western Balkans countries as a guarantee of stability, economic development and social progress both in South-Eastern Europe and across the European continent as a whole.

Bulgaria took concrete steps and initiatives by, inter alia: supporting reforms in the candidate countries so as to meet the membership criteria more quickly; pushing for stronger involvement from the region's countries in achieving the EU's strategic goals; and maintaining a strong focus on connectivity both amongst the candidate countries and between them and the member states of the region in all its dimensions—transport, energy, economy, communication, digitalisation and facilitating people-to-people contacts. The final document from the summit in Sofia confirmed the EU's political will for expansion into the Western Balkans. Efforts have been made to accompany this document with a Roadmap detailing specific initiatives, commitments and indicative deadlines for their implementation.

In addition, Bulgaria sought to increase the Black Sea region's visibility, including increasing connectivity with the Danube region. This presidency of the Council of the EU will be remembered for its key ideas: the future; opportunity; a European perspective; and connectivity in the Balkans. Bulgaria is proud to have succeeded in bringing the European perspective of Western Balkans countries to the forefront of the EU's agenda. The Bulgarian Presidency made efforts for the General Affairs Council to come to an agreement on deciding to open negotiations with Macedonia, as well as injecting a positive tone for consideration of Albania.

The North Macedonia Case

In November 2020, Bulgaria stated that it would not support the negotiating framework for North Macedonia, given that Skopje was violating the 2017 Treaty of Friendship. However, if the green light was ultimately to be given, this would happen only upon clarification of certain questions about common history and language in accordance with three specific conditions: adherence to the 1999 language formula; provision of a road map for the Treaty's implementation and acceptance that claims for a Macedonian minority in Bulgaria will not be supported. At the same time, Bulgaria did, though, approve membership negotiations with Albania.

With these demands, Bulgaria aims to achieve the same arrangements that all divided Balkan nations share with their brother nations, as already exist between Greece and Cyprus, Serbia and its related republics, Albania and Kosovo, as well as Romania and Moldova. Looking somewhat further afield, a similar understanding also exists between Germany and Austria.

For Bulgaria, the two main issues are language and general history. Any change to the constitution so as include citizens who self-identify as Bulgarians is clearly a sovereign decision for North Macedonia, but its actual implementation is necessary to maintain momentum in the negotiations. This difficulty stems from the fact that issues related to Bulgaria directly affect the Macedonian people's self-determination. As such, 2030 is an ambitious, but not unrealistic deadline for completing negotiations and implementing the Republic of North Macedonia's entry into the EU.

What to Do with Ukraine?

Even if Ukraine received a European perspective from the European Commission, it is clear that in its current shape (economic, political and institutional) the present European Union would struggle with acceptance. Of course, Ukraine and its citizens need as much support as possible in this difficult situation, such as weapons, money, humanitarian aid and political backing. Hence, an invitation is the most important signal that the EU can send. However, this has triggered some level of public opposition in Bulgaria, led by Russian-backed narratives and parties that share pro-Russian sentiments, which neither support the accession of Ukraine to the EU nor the actions of the EU towards Russia. Conversely, Bulgaria is interested in the accession of Ukraine and Moldova, since there have been large Bulgarian communities there since the nineteenth century. Whilst overall public opinion certainly supports any efforts directed at helping Ukraine, nevertheless the hesitant political elite do not endorse that position.

Recommendations

From the perspective of enlargement, there is a clear need for institutional change. Mandatory unanimity that is currently blocking various decisions (especially those related to enlargement) must finally be dropped in favour of a majority voting system.

Some strategic effort in changing Bulgarian perceptions and reservations regarding further EU expansion needs to be forthcoming. It is time for all fears of overspending and other repercussions to be put aside. Pressure on national governments towards achievement of policy-based interactions with neighbours must be applied and maintained. A quick, evidence-based success story might work to change frozen attitudes towards enlargement. Moreover, a positive commitment and continued pressure towards the necessary reforms in order to establish firm economic growth agenda is required.

For all this to succeed, though, it is necessary to deepen cohesion between the economies of current member states before moving on to enlargement. Otherwise, EU expansion will include too many poor countries, which will be costly not only in financial terms, but also potentially for the EU's future.

Ivan Nachev , Ph.D., is a Bulgarian political scientist at the New Bulgarian University and an expert on the European Union's political integration. His interests are in the fields of political theory and practice, European values, European integration theories, strategies and political practices. He is a member of the Bulgarian Association for Political Sciences, the Institute for Public Policies and Partnership, the European Community Studies Association (ECSA) and Team Europe at the European Commission.

Hristo Panchugov , Ph.D., is Assistant Professor in the Department of Political Science at the New Bulgarian University, and is a graduate from the Central European University (Hungary).

The New Bulgarian University was established in 1991 following a resolution by the Bulgarian Parliament. Its mission is to be an autonomous liberal education institution dedicated to the advancement of university education by offering accessible and affordable opportunities for interdisciplinary and specialised education as well as high quality research. The University is also a member of TEPSA.

Croatia: Between Proclaimed Enthusiasm and Reality on the Ground

Hrvoje Butković

Achievements Within the Given Framework

Croatia was the first Stabilisation and Association Process country that successfully concluded European Union (EU) accession negotiations and joined the Union. Its governments have always viewed continuation of EU enlargement as an important factor in bringing stability to the Western Balkan region. The reasons for this support are both economic and political, given that three of the Western Balkan countries share with Croatia the longest external land border of any EU Member State. If one were to pick a topic for which the 2020 Croatian Presidency of the Council of the EU pledged most, then that would be further enlargement in the Western Balkans, at which point the Council of the EU reached agreement on a new enlargement methodology. This directly prompted the opening of accession talks with Albania and North Macedonia.

Support for the continuation of enlargement in Croatia is not just an issue driven by its political and economic elites. Results from the 2022 Eurobarometer survey corroborate similar results from previous years by indicating strong public support for enlargement among Croatian citizens, with 72% of Croatians surveyed saying that they support further enlargement, well above the EU level average of 47%.

From its inception in 2014 Croatia was a member of the Berlin Process. Since that time, this format has become a leading initiative and the most prominent driving force behind the enlargement process, aimed at encouraging regional cooperation and cross-sectoral integration. The Prespa agreement between Greece and North Macedonia signed in 2018 was one of the highlights of this Process, resolving a long-standing dispute over Macedonia's name. Among economic successes, the 2020 Common Market Initiative should be underlined with its aim of creating a four freedoms regional market within the Western Balkans.

H. Butković (✉)
The Institute for Development and International Relations, Zagreb, Croatia
e-mail: butkovic@irmo.hr

Nevertheless, despite its achievements the Berlin Process clearly suffers from structural shortcomings which states involved should aspire to overcome. The most important refer to the non-existent monitoring and evaluation mechanisms as well as the legally non-binding nature of its agreements and declarations. Yet, as with other States involved, Croatia does not seem to work on upgrading and reforming this important initiative.

Paradoxes of State Positions

Looking more closely at Croatia's policy towards the region, it is possible to observe some inconsistencies between proclaimed goals and the true situation on the ground. In 2008 and 2009 Slovenia blocked Croatia's EU accession due to a dispute over the maritime border in the Gulf of Piran. At that time Croatian officials provided statements of assurance that once in the EU Croatia would not behave similarly towards other aspiring regional countries. Yet, ever since its 2013 accession Croatia has taken advantage of the right to veto any opening of new negotiating chapters in Serbia's and Montenegro's EU accession process, largely because of unresolved border issues, thus reminiscent of Slovenia's behaviour towards Croatia from some 15 years earlier. It is regrettable that today more than 30 years since dissolution of the former Yugoslavia this issue still remains unsettled.

At the heart of this current enlargement stalemate lies the paradox that expanding the EU acquis imposes transformative costs on the Western Balkans countries which are much higher than in the previous enlargement rounds. At the same time, though, these countries are among the most underdeveloped countries that have ever aspired toward EU Membership. For example, in 2022 the GDP per capita in Bulgaria, as one of least developed EU Member States, was USD 12,505 per capita, while in Albania it was USD 6369. In order to overcome this paradox, a country such as Croatia must come up with innovative initiatives designed to pull this process out of its current stagnation, which unfortunately has not happened to date.

Croatia strongly supports the so-called individualised approach to enlargement so far as the Western Balkans are concerned. It is based on the logic that each aspiring Member State should be evaluated individually and it strays away from any idea of collective enlargement towards the region as such. Nevertheless, the fact that 10 years after enlargement to Croatia, we do not find any new Members from the Western Balkans on the horizon, does not speak in favour of this traditional approach. The idea of a fast-track collective enlargement to the entire Western Balkan region has been promoted by Croatian political scholar Dejan Jović, but in political and broader academic circles this is still considered controversial.

Recommendations

In the circumstances where the EU enlargement policy finds itself in deep crisis, Croatia has the political and moral obligation to become more proactive concerning its reform and reconceptualization. Today this is needed more than ever before, because Ukraine, Moldova and Georgia are now also on the road to EU Membership and Croatia fully supports their efforts.

This chapter has shown that while often being branded as one of the most pro-enlargement EU Member States, Croatia has ample room to become even more constructive. In order to speed up the Western Balkan countries' path towards EU Membership, Croatia should show more political will towards resolving numerous open border issues with its neighbours. Its initiatives do not need to be all-encompassing, but the country must show that it has both a capacity and willingness to move the enlargement agenda forward. Technically and conceptually upgrading the Berlin Process may represent a good initial step for the affirmation of Croatia as a genuine promoter of enlargement.

Hrvoje Butković , Ph.D., works as a Senior Research Associate at the Institute for Development and International Relations (IRMO) Zagreb. The topics of his scientific interest are development of democracy at the national and supranational level together with industrial relations in an internationally comparative perspective.

The Institute for Development and International Relations (IRMO), Zagreb, is a public, non-profit, scientific research organisation engaged in multidisciplinary research. It provides strategic decision support and analysis to decision makers and ensures dissemination of research results and information through publishing activities.

The National Debate in Cyprus on the Future of EU Enlargement Policy

Giorgos Kentas

Nicosia is clearly supportive of European Union (EU) enlargement in the West Balkans and Eastern Neighbourhood. According to the latest Eurobarometer survey (summer 2022), 58% of Cypriots support further expansion to include other countries in future. However, at the same time Cyprus is concerned with the broader implications of a larger Union. Within the national debate some issues are puzzling, such as how far and how fast the EU can grow. Does the EU need to reconsider this process and the various stages of its enlargement policy? Does it need a new institutional framework or even a new Treaty? Would it be able to function effectively as a Union of 35 or more Member States? What are the implications of slower growth? How would small states such Cyprus be affected within a larger Union?

There is widespread concern that a larger Union may diminish the ability of small states to protect vital national interests, given that they pursue EU membership as a means of protection from the arbitrary use of power by larger states. The EU may not constitute a system of collective security *vis-à-vis* external military threats, but it certainly offers an extensive security net of solidarity and support, while preserving equal rules and procedures for all Member States. Could that system be preserved if the EU were to grow further?

Cypriots are generally well-informed about various challenges that relate to the EU's enlargement policy regarding both opportunities and limitations. Opinion-makers suggest that the current historic contingency engenders some new strategic implications of EU enlargement; namely, the war in Ukraine has brought about a major rethinking about European security and defence policy. EU enlargement is the Union's largest security project and it comes as no surprise that vulnerable states such as Ukraine, Georgia and Moldova are seeking membership. In that context, the EU's enlargement policy is back on the agenda; it emerges as an issue of peace, security and stability for the whole Europe. It is a policy that manifests the very

---

G. Kentas (✉)
University of Nicosia – Cyprus Centre for International Affairs, Nicosia, Cyprus
e-mail: kentas.g@unic.ac.cy

values on which EU Member States stand united to defend: democracy; economic stability and prosperity; human rights; the rule of law; and international law.

Being victims of a similar international crime, Türkiye's invasion of Cyprus in 1974 that has resulted in a 49-years-long military occupation and a de facto division of the island as well as its people, Cypriots stand strongly behind the candidacies of European countries that seek security, stability and prosperity within the EU family. Public surveys show that the people of Cyprus appreciate their own country's admission into the EU and expect the maximum solidarity and support by the Union and its Member States not only in re-uniting their island, but also defending their sovereignty against external challenges and provocations.

Two Major Positions

The politics of EU enlargement is embedded in Cyprus' national debate. There are two dominant positions, which seem to reflect wider discussion across the Union. On the one hand, certain sceptics are not enthusiastic about a so-called fast-track enlargement, citing the issue of EU conditionality. They suggest that candidate countries and countries eligible for opening accession negotiations must be dealt with in accordance with their individual circumstances. To be granted membership, these countries must show commitment in meeting the EU acquis by pursuing the necessary reforms and adopting Union policies. Accession is portrayed as a long and demanding process that entails responsibility and commitment.

These sceptics point to problems that emanate from existing Member States, which test the Union's cohesion and Member States' ability to identify common interests. The rejection of bids from Romania and Bulgaria to join Schengen in December 2022, when Austria and the Netherlands voted against—citing concerns that they were ineffective in tackling illegal migration—is one example raised to indicate problems of coordination in a Union of 27 Member States. Sceptics also refer to rule of law problems in some EU countries, suggesting that admitting new countries should be undertaken cautiously.

Conversely, there is a group of enlargement enthusiasts who believe that EU conditionality could be relaxed in the interests of European security amid a complex geopolitical context. Political and social figures in Cyprus suggest that the enlargement policy must be reimagined, become more creative and answer to the challenges that lie ahead. They bring forward some facts for consideration. This year marks the 50th anniversary since the European Communities was first enlarged in 1973. Ever since, 22 European countries have joined the Union with only one, the United Kingdom, having left in 2020. It is already 10 years since the last round of EU enlargement in 2013, when Croatia joined the Union. Today, there are seven European countries holding the status of candidate for EU membership (Ukraine, Moldova, Albania, Serbia, Montenegro, North Macedonia and Türkiye). Georgia along with Bosnia and Herzegovina applied in 2022 and 2016, respectively, albeit only the latter received the status of candidate country. These countries were reassured many times that the EU is seriously committed to their admission to the

Union, but no date for accession has yet been given. Numerous meetings and conferences were held between EU and Western Balkan candidate states; however, there is still no breakthrough in moving the process to an ultimate result.

Further delay in EU enlargement offers geopolitical space for actors such as China and Russia to partner with Western Balkan countries. In addition, Türkiye, a country that applied for EU membership in 1987 and opened accession negotiations in 2005, continues to distance itself from the Union and pursue a revisionist foreign policy that threatens regional and European security. Under Erdogan, Türkiye is sliding into an authoritarian regime with massive violation of democratic principles, human rights and political liberties. Instead of behaving as a prospective partner, Ankara emerges more as a competitor for the Union in the Western Balkans and Eastern Neighbourhood. Moreover, there are even occasions when Türkiye also undermines certain EU countries' domestic cohesion.

Recommendations

EU enlargement is associated with the Union's power of attraction. Hence, the Union and its Member States need to strike a better balance in promoting community and national interests. Three policy recommendations are put forward here for the EU to contemplate in keeping its enlargement policy on track. Firstly, the interests of candidate countries must be kept alive. To do that, the process of EU enlargement policy needs to be updated so that candidate countries can participate in Union proposals and programmes. Secondly, political elites, entrepreneurs and grassroots groups from candidate countries must feel part of EU integration. The Union needs to create a new space for political cooperation between the EU and candidate countries' societies. Thirdly, the EU needs to expand its framework of a creative and coherent multi-speed Europe in areas where common policies and initiatives could be pursued between EU Member States and candidate states. Reforming the Union's Treaties and/or abandoning unanimity in foreign and security policy, fiscal policy and social policy is much more difficult than creating a framework for sectoral cooperation among EU Member States or among candidate states and EU states.

Traditionally, the EU's enlargement policy is understood mostly as a process between EU institutions and candidate countries. However, in practice it is the interests of certain EU countries and their advanced or special bilateral relations with candidate countries that motivate the latter to stay on the accession path. It is time for EU Member States to assume more active roles in working closely with candidate countries in exchanging good practices, advancing bilateral cooperation and coordinating in the future enlargement framework.

Giorgos Kentas, Ph.D., is Associate Professor in International Politics and Governance at the Department of Politics and Governance at the University of Nicosia. He is Director of a Master Program in Public Administration. His research focuses on strategic management, politics and governance at the national and European level. He follows EU developments and studies their implications for Member States and world politics. Recently he has published a paper on Brexit and its implications for Cyprus and a paper on strategic planning in the public sector of Cyprus.

The University of Nicosia is the largest private university in Cyprus. It offers more than 100 conventional and distance learning online programmes at Bachelor, Master and Doctorate level. It hosts more than 11,500 students from all over the world and it is a member of TEPSA.

The Czech Approach to EU Enlargement: Full Steam Ahead!

Zdeněk Sychra and Petr Kratochvíl

Czechia has traditionally been one of the strongest supporters of further European Union (EU) enlargement. This is not only because the Western Balkans and Eastern Europe are long-term priorities within Czech foreign policy, but also because it is in the country's interests to bring long-term stability to these regions in Czechia's broader neighbourhood. Specifically, the Czech enlargement strategy assumes a more comprehensive approach, as by keeping these states on a trajectory of gradual rapprochement with the EU, it also aims at preventing the strengthening of other actors' influence such as, but not limited to, Russia and China. This approach builds on the region's proximity and strategic importance as well as its familiarity and traditionally good relations with these countries. In the context of war in Ukraine, Czechia increasingly views enlargement as a geostrategic investment. Czech diplomacy believes that enlargement is not just a matter of formally fulfilling the criteria, but that in the new geopolitical situation, the values of belonging to the West are more important than ever. Hence, whereas previously Czech support for enlargement was mainly motivated by economic interests and for some Eurosceptic political elites it was a welcome opportunity to 'dilute' integration, today a values-based attitude prevails.

Z. Sychra (✉)
University of West Bohemia, Plzeň, Czechia
e-mail: sychra@kap.zcu.cz

P. Kratochvíl
Institute of International Relations Prague, Prague, Czechia
e-mail: kratochvil@iir.cz

Strengthening Enlargement, Forgetting the Eastern Partnership

For Czechia, the European future of South Eastern Europe is a way to address various challenges, whether economic or social and ethnic, thus constituting a key priority. Hence, EU enlargement has also been reflected in both Czech Presidencies of the Council of the EU so far during 2009 and 2022. As part of the former, the Eastern Partnership was established as a coherent EU policy towards its eastern neighbours. During the latter, accession negotiations with Albania and North Macedonia were launched and after many years Bosnia and Herzegovina finally gained promotion to candidate status. Czechia also succeeded in reaching a united position in the Council on abolition of the visa regime with Kosovo from 2024 at the latest and accepted its EU application as a presiding State. In the context of candidate countries' deeper involvement in the integration process, Czechia supported the inclusion of Western Balkan representatives and their participation in plenary sessions at the Conference on the Future of Europe (2021-2022).

From the Czech point of view, two main factors complicating the enlargement process can be identified. The first is internal. Granting candidate status to Ukraine and Moldova, which have skipped the potential candidate stage, weakens the political credibility of enlargement. Logically, the Western Balkans feel 'cheated' and find it difficult to find further motivation to support reforms. Hence, Czechia fears that the already fragile conditionality on which the enlargement process is based may crumble. From the Czech and broader Central European perspectives, the Western Balkan countries' integration process is progressing only slowly. This is mainly due to bilateral disputes, which add a sense of frustration in candidate countries, reduce any motivation for desired reforms and weaken the sense of identification with the EU. Bilateral disputes between candidate and Member States thus represent a major obstacle to the enlargement process. The Czech Republic (together with Slovakia) did not hesitate to express its frustration politically by rejecting the European Council conclusions on enlargement in December 2020, when Bulgaria vetoed the opening of accession negotiations with Northern Macedonia. Czechia has had its own experience with such a situation, when a bilateral dispute with Austria over the Temelín nuclear power plant's safety interfered with its accession negotiations.

The second factor is external but closely linked to the first. From a geostrategic point of view the continued slowdown in enlargement threatens to increase other actors' influence, mainly Russia and China (but also Turkey). Yet, the Western Balkans region represents a key area for the EU in terms of energy, migration and security. That is why the Czech government has, inter alia, strongly supported a financial package to reduce the region's energy dependence on Russia. At the same time, Czechia expects the Western Balkan states to share the EU's foreign policy values towards Russia. This includes respect for sanctions, which is particularly in conflict with Serbia's very different approach. Furthermore, the Czech government believes that Russia's attack on Ukraine has started a new dynamic of bringing neighbouring states closer to the EU, as evidenced not only by the granting of candidate status to Ukraine and Moldova, but also by the start of negotiations with Albania and Northern Macedonia. There is a surprisingly strong foreign policy consensus on this strategy which is likely to become even stronger. The only dissenting voice within Czech foreign policy was that of President Miloš Zeman, but his retirement from office in March 2023 will effectively remove this distinctly pro-Serbian approach from the country's politics.

Given this stress on enlargement, it is somewhat surprising that the Czech government has not come up with any initiatives to strengthen the Eastern Partnership and nor has it sought to keep this agenda to the fore, unlike other initiators (Poland and Sweden). In contrast to today's support for Ukraine, the Czech Republic has not even attempted to mediate in the Hungarian-Ukrainian dispute over alleged violations of the Hungarian minority's rights, which escalated in 2018. While any passivity has long gone, especially following Russia's invasion of Ukraine, the absence of a Czech vision for further development of the Eastern Partnership becomes significant. This is especially true in relation to Ukraine, Moldova and Georgia, which are now paradoxically part of both the formally separate enlargement policy and the European Neighbourhood Policy.

Enlargement as a Political Priority, But Marginal for the Public

Unlike the first decade of this century, when enlargement was at the centre of public interest, today it is largely an expert subject with minimal public communication. Czech political parties pay marginal attention to this issue in their election programmes, concentrating instead on other topics which dominate the Czech debate on European policy. This is also reflected in public attitudes. Despite strong government support, the Czech public is much more cautious, although still rather positive about the accession of other countries. Czech support for enlargement is below the EU average, with 51% of Czechs supporting it and 38% opposing (Eurobarometer 2022). Support for granting candidate status to Ukraine is also lukewarm (43% for and 46% against, Eurobarometer 2023). The most important criterion for enlargement from the Czech public's perspective is acceptance of the European value framework and rules, closely followed by the economic dimension. Negative attitudes among the public are thus largely linked to fears of transferring problems from less developed countries to Czechia, either due to the problems with the rule of law (corruption, clientelism, crime) or a weaker economic performance.

On a diplomatic level, support for enlargement is strongly pragmatic in its orientation. Primarily, more stress is put on the need to find an EU-internal consensus about enlargement. Although the Czech government itself is not proposing specific changes, it has shown more openness to discussing partial reforms of the enlargement process, for which the Czech Republic is likely to advocate flexibility. This means involving candidate countries in some policies (such as the Single Market) before full Membership is achieved. Secondly, the need to meet the EU's integration capacity commitments must also be considered. The Czech Republic expects the EU to discuss institutional changes in relation to decision-making processes in more-depth and redefine the use of Qualified Majority Voting as a condition for further enlargement. At the same time, the Czech government is not keen on any major intervention in the EU treaties, nor in abandoning unanimity in the Council in existing areas Thirdly, Czechia's economic position within the EU is changing, with the country slowly but surely moving from a net recipient to a net payer position. Clearly, the accession of new Members will accelerate this process. However, as the Czech economy is heavily export-oriented, this shift may be offset by expansion of the internal market. Moreover, the post-war reconstruction of Ukraine is seen as a huge future opportunity.

Recommendations

From a Czech perspective, the weak link in enlargement appears to be the blocking of individual chapters through bilateral disputes between States. Hence, it is worth considering whether to limit unanimity in an effort to find resolution (use of the Qualified Majority Voting, or to give the European Commission more room for discretionary decisions). Member States have other options to block a candidate's entry at a later stage, either during the approval of the accession treaty in the Council or during national ratification.

The new enlargement methodology introduced in 2020 brings interesting innovative elements to enhance the credibility of enlargement (transparency and citizen participation), but does not define concrete tools to achieve this. This deficit needs to be addressed, especially to strengthen the confidence of citizens on both sides in the progress of Western Balkan countries' integration into the EU.

Regarding public perception of the EU, any argumentation for the accession of other countries based on purely economic reasons is not sufficient; these reasons typically fail in public debate unless the affected side is also acknowledged. The war in Ukraine could therefore act as a specific 'window of opportunity' to improve promotion and explain the meaning of enlargement to the European public.

By granting candidate status to two Eastern European countries, the original purpose of the Eastern Partnership within the European Neighbourhood Policy is being depleted. The Czech government should push for a redesign of this policy within the EU, which would better correspond to the current geopolitical situation in Europe.

Zdeněk Sychra is a member of the Department of Political Science and International Relations, University of West Bohemia and an external associate of the Institute of International Relations Prague. His academic interests include the issues of European politics, the Economic and Monetary Union and political governance in the EU. As an author and co-author, he has published numerous articles and book chapters on European Union politics.

The University of West Bohemia is one of the most visible universities in the Czech Republic. The Department of Politics and International Relations of Faculty of Arts is an academic institution offering a broad range of undergraduate, graduate and postgraduate study programmes, conducting research in political science, international relations and territorial studies.

Petr Kratochvíl is a Senior Researcher of the Institute of International Relations Prague and a Member of the TEPSA Board. He has written dozens of monographs, book chapters and journal articles. His research interests cover theories of international relations, European studies and the religion-politics nexus.

The Institute of International Relations Prague (IIR) is an independent public research institution which has been conducting scholarly research in the area of international relations since 1957. As an institution originally founded by the Ministry of Foreign Affairs of the Czech Republic, the IIR also provides policy analysis and recommendations. It tries to form a link between the academic world, the public and international political practice.

Denmark's Position on Enlargement

Zlatko Jovanovic and Marcus Popov Damgaard

Recent Shifts in Danish Policies and Attitudes Towards the Enlargement

Denmark's position on European Union (EU) enlargement has changed substantially over the last 6 to 7 years. Historically, since it joined the European Community, Denmark had previously shared its position on this issue with the United Kingdom prior to Brexit. The two countries—together with Sweden and Finland after 1995—saw enlargement as an opportunity to benefit economically by entering new markets with easy access to cheap labour in new Member States. Furthermore, enlargement was seen as a tool to ensure political stability, rule of law and democracy in the former Eastern Bloc countries. However, enlargement fatigue after the 2004 and 2007 accessions gradually changed this position, culminating with Brexit when Denmark found itself in a completely new situation without its historical ally. Although not fully sharing the integrationist policies of France and the Netherlands, Denmark has now shifted closer to French and Dutch opposition *vis-à-vis* further enlargement, resulting in blocking at the beginning of accession negotiations with Albania and North Macedonia[1] in 2019. The most widespread argument for this among Danes was that no new country should be accepted into the EU, before it can be guaranteed that it will not become a new Poland or Hungary by not complying with the EU's general policies regarding the rule of law and minority rights. Yet with heightened Chinese activity in the region and Russia's invasion of Ukraine in 2022

---

[1] Another shift worthy of mention here concerns Türkiye. Historically—as with the United Kingdom—Denmark has supported Türkiye's accession to the EU. However, since about 10 to 15 years ago, when speaking of enlargement, Danish public and political elites alike exclusively think Western Balkans. Hence, in this chapter, we will not be dealing with Türkiye. Our focus will be exclusively on Ukraine and the Western Balkans.

Z. Jovanovic (✉) · M. P. Damgaard
Democracy in Europe Information Association, Copenhagen, Denmark
e-mail: Zlatko@deo.dk

© The Author(s), under exclusive license to Springer Nature Switzerland AG 2023
M. Kaeding et al. (eds.), *Enlargement and the Future of Europe*,
https://doi.org/10.1007/978-3-031-43234-7_7

as well as threats to European security, a sense of urgency is starting to influence the EU's approach to enlargement, thereby affecting Denmark's recent reluctance.

Coinciding largely with this Brexit-related shift in the Danish position on enlargement policy, in recent years the EU has experienced growing concern with increasing influences from China, Russia and Türkiye in the Western Balkans, that has introduced a new geopolitical perspective on enlargement, which is largely defined by the Western Balkan countries' geographical location. This new perspective has become central in Denmark and frequently used by those arguing for enlargement. In brief, this argument understands that if the EU keeps Western Balkans countries outside for too long, they may well choose to look to China, Russia and Türqyie. This line of thinking has been further strengthened, since Russia's invasion of Ukraine, once again challenging Denmark's recent apprehension on enlargement, which has now become a necessary geopolitical tool.

The war in Ukraine has brought about a security-political shift towards enlargement. In the last two decades Russia's interests in the Western Balkan region have mostly been political, based on a strategy of increasing Russia's influence by aligning itself to pro-Russian forces in the various countries. This fact gained heightened significance following Russia's invasion of Ukraine on 24 February 2022. Shortly thereafter, on 6 March 2022 as a direct consequence of the war's profound change in the EU's security, a referendum on abolition of the Danish defence opt-out—one of four in total—was announced by the EU. This was decided as part of a broad multi-party defence agreement reached during the first 2 weeks of the invasion. The referendum held on 1 June 2022 gave an overwhelming 'yes' to abolition with two thirds of the votes voting in favour. The first reaction of the Danish Prime Minister Mette Frederiksen was that this vote 'sent a clear signal to Vladimir Putin'.

The overwhelming result of this referendum certainly marks a decisive moment in Danish-EU relations, pointing towards a clearer integrationist stance from both the Danish public and mainstream political parties. At the same time polls showed that almost two thirds of the Danish population supported EU Membership for Ukraine, thus corroborating a general shift in Denmark's attitude. Given that opinion polls showed the most markedly pro-Ukrainian stance in Europe, accepting Ukraine as a Member State could best be explained as comprising a declaration of solidarity combined with a measure of security.

That the case of Ukraine occupies a special place is revealed by a poll undertaken in Winter 2022, before the Russian invasion and Ukraine's status as a candidate country. This showed general opposition to further EU enlargement, with over 50% of respondents expressing opposition. In addition, while the coalition-government in power since December 2022 is taking measures to play a more active part in the EU, the prospects of further enlargement are cited with some reservations in the government's position paper: On the one hand, full emphasis is placed on Danish support for Ukraine's future Membership. However, albeit not mentioning the six other candidate countries directly, it does, on the other hand, present some general reservations about the risk of further expansion without having secured new Member States' adherence to the Union as a community of values.

New Priorities in the Western Balkans

Prior to the Russian invasion of Ukraine, when speaking about EU enlargement, most people in Denmark would think exclusively of the Western Balkans.

Any general apprehension expressed by both the Danish public and politicians referred to the six Western Balkan countries as not being ready for Membership. This was largely grounded in problems concerning the rule of law, corruption, organised crime and a perceived high risk within the public domain of heightened immigration from the countries, should they receive Membership. This position united both the left and right in Denmark, albeit for different reasons: an opinion poll in 2018 showed that 69% of liberal-conservative voters opposed enlargement in the Western Balkans because of ideological opposition to globalisation and fears about the dangers of immigration, whereas 53% of the left opposed enlargement because of social dumping and its risks to the Danish model as well as its welfare state.

While enlargement and the accession process were seen as tools to ensure political stability, the rule of law and democracy in the Western Balkan countries, since at least 2010s, these issues have now become critical. Realistically, political stability has been evaluated as the most important of the three at the expense of democratisation and strengthening the rule of law. In response to Milorad Dodik's repeated threats to internal stability in Bosnia and Herzegovina, Serbia's president Aleksandar Vučić was widely seen as supposedly the best guarantor for peace and stability in Bosnia and Herzegovina and indeed the whole region, despite Serbia experiencing clear democratic backsliding under his government. This position has been taken up by top diplomats in the Danish Foreign Ministry, who at the same time as prioritising importance of the Copenhagen Criteria have expressed confidence and trust in Vučić as a necessary stabilising factor, regardless of the negative developments in terms of democracy, press freedom and the rule of law in Serbia. A strategy of prioritising stability over concrete improvements and taking advantage of countries in the accession process has evidently been unproductive. This becomes especially obvious when according to Denmark none of the candidate countries were deemed eligible to join the EU, according to Prime Minister Mette Frederiksen when asked at the last Western Balkans summit in October 2021.

However, after the Russian invasion there has been a necessary change in security priorities. When his government rejected the imposition of sanctions on Russia during 2022, Vučić came under strong criticism, which posed a threat to the region's security. Moreover, in many ways this intensified the focus on Russia's regional interests, representing a dramatic change in priorities with geo-strategic issues regarding Russia coming to the fore, replacing the previous concentration on internal factors in the Western Balkans. With Russian interests prompting such urgency for re-establishing political priorities, this could potentially accelerate the Western Balkans accession process, bringing about yet new ways of marginalising the apprehensive stance on enlargement, a position that in many ways informs Denmark's approach. While the EU—now maybe more than ever—should play a stability and security-political role in the region, this must not be done at the expenses of democratic reforms relating to the accession processes. Otherwise, democratic backsliding could—as in the Serbian case—return like a pendulum, producing stability problems in the region.

Recommendations: Learning from Previous Examples

Compared with Bulgaria and Romania, Croatia has been doing somewhat better since it became Member of the EU in 2013. This has much to do with the Croatian and Romanian-Bulgarian respective accession process, where according to various Croatian NGOs and analysts, a crucial period of Croatia's democratisation process occurred while the country was negotiating Membership with the EU. This indicates that the EU has opportunities to influence democratisation in the Western Balkans, as well as Ukraine and Moldova, during these accession processes. Accordingly, Denmark should now replace its apprehensive stance with a focus on the rule of law, democracy and corruption.

However, spurring democratisation and the rule of law in the Western Balkans (and Ukraine) can be fulfilled only by taking the candidate countries under specific consideration. Opinions expressed by Western Balkans candidate countries is that they are currently paying for mistakes of the past, for instance the reversal of democratisation after Poland and Hungary gained Membership. It is crucial that Denmark pushes for genuinely rewarding the candidates once concrete improvements are made, as opposed to the case of North Macedonia.

Finally, it is vital that the new external security priorities *vis-à-vis* Russia's and China's interests in the region do not create a relapse into support for 'stabilitocratic' leaders. Although solidarity with Ukraine and stability in the Western Balkans is crucial, the long-term perspective of the region's candidate countries as well as Ukraine and Moldova should be on democratisation.

Zlatko Jovanovic, Ph.D., is Senior Analyst at Democracy in Europe (DEO). He holds a PhD in Yugoslav history from University of Copenhagen and has taught at the universities of Copenhagen and Aarhus. Jovanovic is author of *A Cultural History of the 1984 Winter Olympics: The Making of Olympic Sarajevo*.

Marcus Popov Damgaard is Project Manager and Communications Officer at Democracy in Europe (DEO). He holds a master's degree in history of ideas from Aarhus University, current editor-in-chief at the Danish webzine on the Eastern European, post-socialist and -soviet countries, Magasinet rØST.

Democracy in Europe Organisation (DEO) is a Danish liberal adult education organisation working for democracy in Europe striving to engage the general public in a nuanced debate on European politics and on the European Union. Following a participatory democratic mind-set, our aim is to activate as many as possible in a versatile and open debate about the content and framework of the European Union. We are independent of political parties and EU bodies. We have no specific political agenda but aim to raise political questions, address problems and discuss European issues in our debates.

Estonia: Supporting Fast-Track Enlargements

Viljar Veebel

The geopolitical situation in Europe impacted by Russian aggression against Ukraine offers a unique opportunity for the European Union (EU) to enlarge geographically, which in turn increases the prospects for deepening integration in terms of security and defence. For many decades now, geopolitical pressures and various associated risks have continued to stimulate citizens' motivation for enlargement, given that additional integration can contribute to regional peace. Particularly from a security perspective, present needs certainly highlight not only the challenges, but also opportunities for the EU to become a more global player.

Is the Union Ready for Geopolitical Enlargement?

One could even go so far as to suggest that there has never been a more opportune time, mindful of the existing experience and well-tested pre-accession procedures. Most candidates this time (excepting Türkiye, Ukraine and Serbia) present cases that are no more complicated than those during the time of Irish or Greek accessions. What is needed, though, are more tailor-made solutions which will help to avoid any complications experienced in the past.

Looking at the bigger picture, European integration needs deepening and widening, both politically and geographically as the process would lose its momentum and advantages without periodic enlargement. From a purely Estonian standpoint, accession talks must be considered as an active counterstrategy to Russian (and Chinese) neo-imperial policies in Ukraine, Moldova and Georgia. So far Russia can be seen as winning the competition for greater influence here, mainly because positive views about EU Membership have been lacking. Once convincing arguments and policies

V. Veebel (✉)
Baltic Defence College, Tartu, Estonia
e-mail: Viljar.Veebel@baltdefcol.org

© The Author(s), under exclusive license to Springer Nature Switzerland AG 2023
M. Kaeding et al. (eds.), *Enlargement and the Future of Europe*,
https://doi.org/10.1007/978-3-031-43234-7_8

about future plans become more apparent, political changes and support for EU integration will follow.

For Estonia, EU accession was one of the biggest achievements after independence and certainly a 'game changer' in being able to leave behind the label 'former Soviet State'. Accordingly, Estonian politicians are ready to support other small States which seek to emulate this achievement as a means of removing their former communist satellite tag. There is only one political party (EKRE Right Wing Radicals) in Estonia, which openly criticises the European integration process, not only by opposing future enlargement, but also in trying to fracture the existing Union.

However, there are also choices to be made for the EU and its Member States. A first dilemma appears as Estonia (and probably the EU generally) would welcome enlargement which can be seen not only as strictly conditionality-based, but also as succeeding. Currently, for those candidate States who really need and want accession, the existing pre-accession procedure is overly time-consuming and too demanding to be believable as a stable political priority which will prevail despite changing governments. This is not just to do with Ukraine, Moldova and Georgia. North Macedonia and Kosovo would also need a faster track to avoid falling back and being attracted by Russian or Chinese alternatives. How to achieve this is here a relevant question. Certainly, more funds should be directed to creating greater motivation with a higher number of EU experts supporting every single candidate country.

In terms of pre-accession positive conditionality, responsibility for the most part rests with the European Commission, the Council of the EU and the European Council. It is the EU, not candidate countries, who can lead with their experience, competence and resources for enlargement, so let them choose on what to focus and how to achieve pre-accession quickly and effectively. However, first some supporting political consensus needs to be found. Despite the European Council's statement that there is a need for 'fair and rigorous conditionality and the principle of own merits', not much advice has been given since the last enlargement that can be considered as helpful in practical terms.

From the perspective of candidate countries, existing conditionality is complicated in two regards. Firstly, accession criteria are in most cases politically assessed and not clearly measurable as benchmarks. Furthermore, progress is assessed only by the Commission itself, without any access to explanations or impartial assessment. As there is a long list of sub-components under each broader criterion, progress report writers can find sufficient justification for any political preference. Hence, in this aspect additional steps in terms of impartial assessment, with transparent success benchmarks and impartial evaluators would help both the candidates and evaluators. Secondly, the criteria need to be realistically fulfillable within a 10-year timeframe. It is virtually impossible to generate long-term stable political commitment from the governments of candidate States, if the process itself takes more than two or three electoral cycles and needs to be a political priority for that entire time. Accordingly, if the conditionality, criteria and accession process have evolved as too complex and time-consuming even for the best possible candidates, then the motivation for change and reform to achieve simplification needs to come from the EU side.

The European Neighbourhood Policy's role needs to be clarified as soon as possible, both in present day terms and how it will be shaped during the pre-accession process. One universal size and road-map can certainly not be applied to all candidates. At least two options will be appropriate for those who: (a) neither want nor qualify for Membership; or (b) are seen as possible future Members, but not yet ready for the full pre-accession process. This qualification would ease both strategic and internal communication for both sides.

What solutions could result for Türkiye, Ukraine and Serbia? These three large candidate/potential candidate countries are viewed as very complex cases from an Estonian perspective, albeit for different reasons. This does not imply Estonia's rejection, but is rather a call for better preparedness and transparency regarding the accession process and ensuing partnership. For Türkiye and Serbia, their willingness to make the necessary political and economic changes stand out as central questions, at least under the current governments. Whilst consideration of these two countries will be challenging, this must not create any delay in assessing other prospective candidates.

The Ukrainian case is of course possibly the most problematic. The country has lost almost half of its GDP and millions of citizens have been displaced because of Russia's invasion. Hence, unprecedented levels of EU support will be needed long before the accession process can be initiated. Ukraine will undoubtedly need a specific strategy for war recovery first from the EU side, whilst at the same time keeping the accession option open. However, belief in their having realistic accession prospects would clearly not only boost Ukraine's fight for its continued independence, but also support the efforts of Moldova and Georgia in their committing to EU accession. For these countries political dialogue or even a light version of Membership will not suffice. Only full Membership would generate sufficient motivation and momentum to drag them out Russia's sphere of influence.

However, does the EU perhaps need further institutional reform, before kicking off a new round of enlargement? For instance, debates over fair distribution of seats in institutions have always been there and will continue to be so during the next enlargement phase. Any institutional reform towards simplification and transparency would certainly be welcomed by Estonia (more seats or votes are not expected) irrespective of enlargement. Indeed, following Brexit there is a lot of free space within the institutions and hence upcoming enlargement should at least in this regard be less complicated. Ukraine and Türkiye as the most populous prospective Members will also raise some institutional concerns, but as stated earlier this should not block the accession process with smaller and motivated candidates. Regarding deeper integration in new policy areas and a growing EU budget, more is viewed as better by the latest version of a policy document titled 'Estonian EU priorities'.

Turning to the EU as a security provider for newcomers, for Georgia, Ukraine and Moldova the EU's ability to play an important role in the security and defence domain is a crucial component. In this aspect the Russo-Ukrainian war can be regarded as inspirational in terms of what could be expected. The EU does not need to copy or replace NATO assets and obligations. The advanced European strategic autonomy should be centred on an ability to make the best out of EU funds for threatened states, both Member States and candidate countries. The EU should be ready to coordinate, prepare and supply necessary military and civilian resources, taking away the necessity for every single Member State to deal bilaterally with concerns related to donations and offers of support, which could be presented as an argument not to seek EU Membership.

Enlargement and the Future of the EU

Historical experience and theoretical knowledge both support the idea that integration is a never-ending process with ever deeper and wider reach, including geographical space. Neo-functional theory also claims that the effects of integration are larger when the starting difference is larger. Of course, Estonia can accept the EU without further enlargement, but integration is seen as an ever-growing and self-creating process, in which enlargement is a necessary component.

Recommendations

Estonia's own experience of accession to the EU clearly speaks in favour of enlargement even during difficult times, which is seen as the best way for small States to move on from the legacy of former communist States, such as the Soviet Union and the Yugoslavian Federation. Estonia is not in any way nationalistic and nor is there a belief that only certain selected nations are worthy of belonging to the EU. Estonian society while having rather vague knowledge about living standards and the accession readiness of Western Balkan states has a mostly positive attitude, even in the face of religious differences, albeit Serbia with its current political preferences is seen as a potentially problematic candidate. During its own accession process, Estonia was not only in favour of EU positive conditionality based on Copenhagen Criteria, but also even seeking more specific and measurable criteria and procedures. In fulfilling pre-accession conditionality, candidate countries' limitations are known and hence any lowering of the bar for geopolitical reasons now implies political decisions.

It is up to the EU and its institutions to find the motivation and momentum for re-vitalising the enlargement process by using this current geopolitical situation where Europeans are ready for enlargement if it helps to secure the region. More transparency is needed from the EU side, in terms of which countries have immediate or long-term Membership aspirations and what they need to do to improve their progress towards qualification.

Existing Member States can serve as role models for specific applicants (as Denmark did for Estonia in its pre-accession process). For every applicant there are specific inducements that would help to convert enlargement into a key political priority.

Many candidates, especially former Soviet republics, see the accession criteria and process as being too long and complicated to form part of a reasonable policy agenda. For those countries which are facing serious strategic choices, a less complex and more individualised approach is needed. Costs and necessary efforts would be bigger from the EU side, but also the chances of success would increase.

In looking at how to boost reforms in candidate countries, Estonia's experience suggests that the best combination is a range of generous financial assistance, measurable and achievable criteria and a strong team of professional experts-advisers from the EU side. Quite simply, if countries cannot find ways of making progress towards meeting accession criteria, then no financial support will be forthcoming. The formula should be that any EU pre-accession funds must be enough to attract all political powers and best experts, all of which must be well secured against corruption.

Viljar Veebel, Ph.D., is a Researcher at the Department of Political and Strategic Studies of the Baltic Defence College and a National Researcher for the European Council on Foreign Relations (ECFR). He has worked as an Academic Advisor for the Estonian government in the European Future Convention and as a researcher for OSCE, SIDA, Estonian Foreign Policy Institute and Eurasia Group. His main research interests include European security and defence initiatives, use of economic sanctions as a foreign policy tool, EU-Russia relations and related sanctions.

The Baltic Defence College is a modern, future-oriented, attractive and competitive, English language-based international defence college with a regional focus and Euro-Atlantic scope. The College serves as a Professional Military Education institution teaching at the operational and strategic levels, applying latest educational principles, effective management and best use of intellectual and material resources.

Finland Should Focus on EU Reforms Ahead of Enlargement

Juha Jokela

During the early years of its European Union (EU) Membership, Finland was supporting both enlarging and deepening of the Union, despite public support for the former remaining relatively low. However, Eastern enlargement and various EU crises over the past decades have brought about a more cautious approach among policy-makers. Nevertheless, Finland has continued to support the EU's enlargement efforts in the Western Balkans, albeit further accessions are seen as resulting from a gradual process reflecting commitment and progress in respective countries. Russia's war of aggression against Ukraine has certainly elevated enlargement questions in Finland's EU agenda. New major eastern enlargement is being approached as a longer-term process and until recently Finland has shied away from discussing necessary EU reforms.

Given Finland's track-record on EU enlargement and reforms, expertise related to the security challenges of the EU's eastern and West Balkans neighbours, as well as good governance, the country is well placed to make a notable contribution to the next accession wave. This certainly requires openness in considering EU enlargement process changes.

Pro-Enlargement Governments, Yet Sceptic Citizens

Finland's positive stance towards EU enlargement is often highlighted in connection with its first EU Presidency in 1999, during which the European Council meeting in Helsinki agreed on further preparations for Eastern enlargement and granted Türkiye applicant status for EU Membership. Importantly, the country also supported EU deepening and backed the transfer of competences to Union level as well as expansion of Qualified Majority Voting in consecutive Treaty reforms during the

---

J. Jokela (✉)
Finnish Institute of International Affairs, Helsinki, Finland
e-mail: Juha.Jokela@fiia.fi

1990s and 2000s. Finland's role in Western Balkans crisis management and mediation at this time underlined its efforts to support peace and stability in the region, including its integration into the EU.

During the past decade, Finland has though displayed symptoms of enlargement fatigue, along with other EU Member States and institutions. While Eastern enlargement has generally been seen as a positive development in Helsinki, democratic backsliding in Hungary and the rule of law challenges in Poland have contributed to a more cautious approach. This change was already visible in 2013, when Finland was ready to block the entry of Bulgaria and Romania into the Schengen Area against the recommendations of the European Commission. The Finnish position reflected concerns related to the endurance of reforms being undertaken in those two countries, as well as a weakening of EU tools to influence developments after full accession to Schengen. Similar points have frequently been raised in conjunction with the 2004/2007 enlargement in general with its negative implications on the EU's efficiency in decision-making, especially regarding the Common Foreign and Security Policy (CFSP).

Re-politicisation of EU matters since the Eurozone crisis as well as the emergence of an openly populist and Eurosceptic party—the Finns Party—as a notable political force in Finland, has also reduced the traditionally pro-European parties' appetite, such as the centre-right National Coalition Party and Social Democrats, to discuss and promote further enlargement. Significantly, the electorate generally has also displayed reservations towards Eastern enlargement. According to a national poll only 24% of Finns viewed enlargement positively in 2001 and by 2006 this had reduced to 19%.

Sea of Change in Attitudes, Yet Not in EU Policy

However, Russia's war of aggression has brought about a significant change in public opinion concerning EU enlargement. This is manifested by a strong support for Ukraine's EU Membership. While in 2016 22% of Finns considered that Ukraine would be a suitable EU Member State in the future, by 2022 this had increased dramatically to 59%, with only 13% against. Despite some variation in terms of demographic and regional factors, this support has increased across different groups and regions.

The government has also taken a positive stance towards Ukraine's Membership, yet it is seen as resulting from a long-term process. There also seems to be an increasing awareness that moving forward with Ukraine and Moldova as well as potentially with Georgia has implications for the Western Balkans, with the countries already in accession negotiations rightly expecting that more attention will now be directed towards their stalled negotiations.

Nevertheless, despite an increasing awareness being provoked by the topicality of EU enlargement, there is very little change in Finland's approach. The government suggests that carefully managed enlargement is in Finland's political and economic interests; hence, it is one of the central objectives of Finland's EU policy. In this respect, experts have noted that given the increasing strategic competition among major powers, the EU's Single Market could turn out to be ever more important for Finland's export-driven economy. Enlarging the Single Market could bring about positive economic effects during times of increasing worries related to free trade and rules-based order. At the same time, Finland underlines that legal matters and the fight against organised crime as well as corruption must remain at the core of the EU's enlargement policy. In terms of key economic indicators, such as growth, competitiveness and management of general government finances as well as a well-functioning public administration, sound reforms and preparedness for the Membership are also highlighted.

The government also maintains that there is no room for compromise regarding accession criteria because becoming a Member State is essentially linked to adoption of the Union's rules and values. Accordingly, Finland holds that accession should not be advanced for (geo)political reasons and that candidate countries' bilateral conflicts must first be ironed out. Regarding the EU, Finland emphasises that it must adhere to its commitments and be willing to accept new Member States when they meet the Membership criteria.

Recommendations

Finland's positive official stance as well as public support towards EU enlargement and an increasing awareness of these future processes' significance for the Union provides a good basis for active engagement in this key policy field. This will though require openness to evaluate and review the EU's enlargement policy.

Firstly, security and geopolitics matter for EU enlargement. Russia's war of aggression against Ukraine speaks volumes about working towards a European perspective for any neighbouring State *without* adequate attention and actions being directed towards security challenges of the country in question. Enlargement makes no sense if it can be denied by an external actor using military force. Moreover, focusing solely on political and economic matters can render a candidate country vulnerable to external aggression.

Secondly, given that accession is often a long-term transformative process, Finland could ponder the possibilities of a so-called step-by-step enlargement. That is, the EU could further revise its negotiation doctrine based on an idea that nothing is agreed before everything is agreed. Candidate countries could be allowed to participate in policy fields, within which they already meet key criteria. This could help those countries sustain their motivation for reforms in the context of long-term accession processes, especially as full rights are reserved for Members, including participation in decision-making.

Finally, the EU must be ready to reform itself in readiness for a new major enlargement. Accordingly, Finland should not shy away from discussions on required Treaty reforms. Early engagement would enable Helsinki to highlight its key proposals for a Treaty change. During the past years Finland has underlined effective EU decision-making in the CFSP and more broadly, as well as new tools to secure EU's common values enshrined in Article 2 of the Treaty. Should the extension of Qualified Majority Voting to the CFSP via a 'passerelle' clause turn out to be too ambitious objective for the Member States, a Treaty change preventing blocking behaviour by one or a few Members could be promoted. Even if the new rule of law mechanism attached to the Multiannual Financial Framework is a step in the right direction, the unanimity rule covering Article 7 sanctions should be re-assessed ahead of enlargement.

Juha Jokela, Ph.D., is Director of the EU and Strategic Competition research programme at the Finnish Institute of International Affairs (FIIA). He was a board member of TEPSA from 2014–2022. His research interests include EU's foreign policy, differentiated integration, Finland's EU policy and the political implications of Brexit.

The Finnish Institute of International Affairs (FIIA) is an independent research institute operating in connection with the Finnish Parliament. The Institute produces high-quality research on international relations, the international economy, the European Union and Finnish foreign policy for use by the academic community, decision-makers and the general public, both nationally and internationally. FIIA is part of TEPSA.

What Infuriating French Reluctance Reveals

Christian Lequesne and Olivier Rozenberg

A striking feature about France's relationship to the European Union (EU) lies in its wanting to limit the number of members, whilst at the same time never questioning its own Membership of the club. From de Gaulle considering the British candidacy as a Trojan horse in 1963 to President Macron opposing the opening of negotiations with Albania and Northern Macedonia in 2019, the continuity is remarkable—as well as the diplomatic priority given to this 'pro small EU' position.

Such continuity results from the fact that this reluctance towards enlargements is rooted in a diversity of mixed claims. Firstly, Eurosceptic forces which have always been present within the French polity regularly take the opportunity to use enlargement as a way of blaming the EU for not protecting national interests enough. This was true not only of the right wing's concerns with competition from Spanish and Portuguese agricultures during the 1980s, but also the left being obsessed with the 'Polish plumber' in the 2000s.

Secondly, and more specific to the French case, enlargements have also been a source of concern for pro-European supporters. The issue can be sketched through opposition between the views expressed by two fathers of European integration: Jean Monnet and Robert Schuman. For the former, Europe was a project of liberalisation and prosperity designed for the entire Western world, beyond France's immediate neighbours. For the latter, the heart of the integration was the Rheinish world from which he originated. In that perspective, adding new Members remote from the French and German geographical areas runs the risk of dissolving the bloc's cohesion.

C. Lequesne
Sciences Po, Paris, France
e-mail: christian.lequesne@sciencespo.fr

O. Rozenberg (✉)
Centre for European Studies and Comparative Politics, Sciences Po, Paris, France
e-mail: olivier.rozenberg@sciencespo.fr

Finally, France's dominant narrative regarding European integration is based largely on the project of restoring France's lost influence worldwide through the diplomatic primacy of a key country within the European polity. Arguably, such leadership capacity could be jeopardised in an EU of 30 or more Members, especially since the Membership of Central and Eastern members de facto would contribute to transferring geographically France to the West rather than the centre of the Union.

Nevertheless, it should be noted that, despite this shared reluctance, French leaders after de Gaulle have pragmatically accepted the enlargement process, stressing on many occasions that enlarging the EU should not prevent its deepening, as if both stood in contradiction.

Continual Reluctance Over Recent Years

As with all French Presidents since the end of the Cold War, President Macron, elected in 2017 and re-elected in 2022, does not have a privileged relationship with Eastern Europe and the Balkans. In addition to the traditional lack of enthusiasm *vis-à-vis* enlargement mentioned above, this can be explained by two specific beliefs among the French foreign policy elites: the region is not seen as a traditional zone of influence for France; and strategic relations with Russia are important. Clear infringements of the rule of law by Hungary and Poland have reinforced French decision-makers' mistrust regarding future enlargements. The bilateral relationship between France and Poland has not been close since Macron came to power in 2017, given that he did not hesitate to criticise openly the Eurosceptic antics of the Polish Law and Justice party. Liberties that governments can take with the rule of law once they are Members of the EU are essential to understanding French reluctance towards enlargement in the Balkans. It is not by chance that in 2019 France was at the origin of a proposal for a new methodology, which subsequently adopted by the 27 Member States in 2021. It both politicises the process by involving the Heads of State and Government to a higher degree, making it easier to stop at any stage and possibly reverse. Similarly, it was France in conjunction with the Netherlands which blocked the opening of accession negotiations with Albania and Northern Macedonia in 2019.

As a result, public opinion also shows reluctance. In the Summer of 2022, the Standard Eurobarometer 97 showed that 46% of French people were against any future enlargement of the EU while 40% were in favour—the EU average being of 57% in favour. Russia's invasion of Ukraine has though played a role in increasing support with 12% more voters now in favour of enlargement compared with 6 months ago. Yet, French citizens remain among the most sceptical in the EU, albeit difficult to separate opposition from indifference as there has never been a real public debate on enlargement to the Balkans, added to which this issue is at present not particularly dominant in political discourse.

A Contemporary Shift?

Regardless of any domestic views, the war in Ukraine has reopened the debate on enlargement at a European level and France cannot afford to ignore that. In June 2022, after a trip to Kyiv with Olaf Scholz and Mario Draghi, Emmanuel Macron endorsed the applications of Ukraine and Moldova, as well as European prospects for Georgia. It was also the French President who in May 2022 proposed that a European Political Community should be convened in order to present a continental reflection on the strategy towards Ukraine. French authorities exerted much effort in explaining that this large network consists in an exercise which is totally independent from enlargement.

Regarding the Balkans, a new official discourse on France's commitment to the area can be observed, albeit it remains marked by minimum service and carefully avoids mentioning enlargement as a political priority. At the 2022 EU-Balkans Summit in Tirana, while the EU Declaration speaks of support for the enlargement process, this is never explicitly mentioned in President Macron's statements. France remains genuinely ambivalent over the Balkans issue. On the one hand, it feels that enlargement is back on the agenda for geopolitical reasons linked to the strong competition from Russia, China and Türkiye in the region. On the other hand, it has no desire to speed up enlargement for fear of bringing in countries that are not respecting the Copenhagen Criteria and hence could subsequently create precisely the same tensions as Orban's Hungary.

Recommendations

Firstly, we call for a broad shift of paradigm among French officials towards enlargement, be they politicians or diplomats. Arguably, any willingness to strengthen 'European sovereignty'—a concept promoted by President Macron—stands in contradiction to enlargement reluctance. A large Europe would geopolitically be more determinant and France would also be more influential within the EU. France must stop opposing enlarging in preference to deepening.

Secondly, France must not consider that enlargement towards the East benefits just Germany and the Central European Member States. A proactive stance with a group of Member States such as Germany and Poland is important as the war in Ukraine continues to shift the EU's centre of gravity towards the East.

Thirdly, some French diplomatic priorities should be adapted to the pro-enlargement mood largely shared by European capitals. This is especially the case regarding the European Political Community: French officials should keep on explaining that this new format is not designed to counter enlargement.

Christian Lequesne, Ph.D., is Professor of Political Science at the Centre for International Research of Sciences Po. He obtained his Ph.D. and later Habilitation in Sciences Po Paris and is specialised in European studies and diplomacy. He is co-founder and co-editor-in-chief of the European Review of International Studies.

Olivier Rozenberg, Ph.D., is Associate Professor in Political Science at the Centre for European Studies and Comparative Politics of Sciences Po. He specialises in the study of European integration and legislature. He has edited several books on those issues and the role of national parliaments in the European integration.

Sciences Po is the leading French research university in Political Science and International Relations. The Centre for European Studies and Comparative Politics is a research centre which was founded at Sciences Po in 2005. With an objective to fulfil three main missions: develop research on European questions at Sciences Po; to facilitate Sciences Po's insertion in European research networks; and to foster the European debate on the future of Europe. The Institute is a member of TEPSA.

Strong Tailwinds for EU Enlargement in Germany: But EU Membership Has a Price Tag

Funda Tekin

Germany's government was not the first to react positively to Ukraine's application for European Union (EU) Membership only 4 days after Russia's full invasion. Indeed, it was not until his joint trip with France's President Emmanuel Macron and Italy's then Prime Minister Mario Draghi to Kyiv in June 2022 that Chancellor Olaf Scholz clearly spoke out in favour of granting Ukraine candidate status.

Three Elements of Germany's Enlargement Policy

However, this initial hesitation does not indicate any fundamental change in Germany's enlargement policy by way of a supporter becoming an opponent. On the contrary, it is an allegory for Germany's approach to EU enlargement, which is determined by three elements.

Firstly, Germany traditionally belongs within the camp of enlargement proponents. This is driven by the geopolitical narrative that a bigger EU will have a greater say not only in Europe, but throughout the world. Moreover, over the past decades there has been parliamentary consensus in the German Bundestag—excluding the right-wing populist party Alternative für Deutschland—that the Western Balkans' future lies within the EU. Consequently, Germany's position on EU enlargement policy has not substantially changed over the years, regardless of governmental party coalitions' composition. The fact that Russia's war of aggression against Ukraine has led to a fundamental geopolitical restructuring in Europe merely enhanced the geopolitical narrative in support of enlargement extending it to the so-called Association Trio, Ukraine, Republic of Moldova and Georgia.

Secondly, Germany puts a clear price tag on EU Membership: no dissolution of the EU, its fundamental values or its acquis communautaire. On behalf of accession

---

F. Tekin (✉)
Institute for European Politics, Berlin, Germany
e-mail: Funda.Tekin@iep-berlin.de

© The Author(s), under exclusive license to Springer Nature Switzerland AG 2023
M. Kaeding et al. (eds.), *Enlargement and the Future of Europe*,
https://doi.org/10.1007/978-3-031-43234-7_11

candidate countries, this requires internal reforms for achieving the accession criteria. On behalf of the EU, 'absorption capacity' has become a determining narrative in German enlargement debates, demanding internal reforms that would equip the EU with institutional structures to function with more than 30 Member States. For Germany, it is very clear that there will be no widening without deepening. Yet, consensus on the sequencing still seems to be lacking. In his speech at the Charles University in Prague in August 2022, Olaf Scholz spoke out in favour of reforming the EU first before granting Membership to additional countries. Other governmental officials voice a less strict opinion on this issue.

Thirdly, enlargement is strongly subjected to domestic politics in Germany. As well as its right to ratify decisions on the accession of new Member States, the German Bundestag can influence Germany's positions at an earlier stage during the accession procedure. Both government and Bundestag are required to find a common position before decisions on granting accession or opening accession negotiations are taken in the Council or European Council. This means that all political parties represented in the Bundestag actively monitor the EU's enlargement policy. Additionally, public opinion represents a crucial factor. Ever since the EU's so-called big bang enlargement involving 12 new Member States in 2004/2007, German public opinion has been sceptical regarding further enlargement rounds. Support for enlargement has ranged between 38% in 2003 and 20% in January 2022. Russia's invasion into Ukraine fundamentally changed this picture. By the summer of 2022, 52% were in favour of enlargement increasing the support rate by about 20% compared to support before the war. Additionally, for the first time in years, the share of respondents in favour of enlargement exceeded that of its opponents.

How to Preserve the Credibility of the EU Enlargement?

In view of these three elements, Germany's approach to addressing a growing sense of the EU's introspection and resultant power vacuum that this opens up to other actors in the Balkans region creates a new focus on (re)establishing credibility for the EU's accession promise. On the one hand, this implies that Germany is keen on preserving the EU's enlargement policy dynamic, given its government's support for the opening of accession negotiations with Albania and North Macedonia as well as granting accession candidate status to Bosnia and Herzegovina.

Turkey, though, currently marks the blind spot in Germany's enlargement policy. EU-Turkey relations have reached rock-bottom. Hence, before Turkish parliamentary and presidential elections that were scheduled for 14 May 2023, the German government has been hesitant to discuss prospects. However, instead of thinking in terms of change, German officials need to prepare for maintaining German- and EU-Turkey relations within a scenario of continuity in the Turkish political system. Furthermore, German officials are slowly starting to consider certain merit-based automatisms in the accession procedure related to integration into the Single Market if respective conditions are met.

On the other hand, Germany initiated the so-called Berlin Process in 2014 and values it as a strong facilitator of the accession process through regional cooperation among the Western Balkans countries in areas of interconnectivity, such as economic cooperation and youth exchange. Germany's perception on the Open Balkan Initiative that focuses on dispersing hurdles on transnational cooperation such as mutual recognition of degrees and work permits though is rather critical, with concerns about the risk of establishing parallel structures.

Berlin is also very vocal on the fact that maintaining credibility for the EU's accession promise additionally entails improving the EU's absorption capacity. The government's coalition agreement in December 2021 put forward a very ambitious EU reform agenda by aiming for a European Convention to follow up the Conference on the Future of Europe, leading to the eventual establishment of a European federation. Today, the government's reform agenda is much more pragmatic, focusing on institutional reforms that might be possible within the existing Treaty framework. In view of an enlarged Union comprising potentially 35+ Member States, the increased use of Qualified Majority Voting seems to be one key condition for maintaining the EU's ability to function. As the government is not a strong supporter of differentiated integration among groups of Member States and/or accession countries, the elimination of veto powers in EU decision-making becomes a priority.

The Impact of the 'Zeitenwende'

To counter military threats on the European continent, it turns out that the 'Zeitenwende' (watershed moment) that Chancellor Olaf Scholz proclaimed only 3 days after Russia's full invasion into Ukraine is anything but a self-fulfilling prophecy. Debates on Germany's contribution to military support for Ukraine and robust defence-capacity building as part of Germany's foreign policy toolbox have been very intense ever since, given the country's still sensitive history of warfare in Europe. Clearly Germany will strengthen foreign, security and defence policy structures, but only within a common European approach which avoids duplications with NATO structures. There will be no German 'Alleingänge' (unilateral actions) in this crucial and critical matter.

Recommendations

Various elements require consideration when Germany and the EU draw up a revised framework for the Union's enlargement policy and the future of Europe. Firstly, timing is a crucial factor. The Western Balkan countries have been at different stages in the accession process for more than 10 years now while Moldova and Ukraine expect a speedy emergency accession. Hence, the EU faces a lot of impatience, but clearly should not yield to pressure and rush decisions. Conversely, the EU should not let the accession process take so long that this undermines candidates' trust in its eventual success and hence its transformative effect. As this implies that it will not be possible for widening to wait for the completion of deepening, a combination of both needs to be sought. The fact that those Member States that tend to oppose internal reforms are also strongly in favour of enlargement represents a starting point for negotiations on a package deal involving deepening and widening.

Secondly, for this to happen Germany's government needs to define its vision of the institutional reforms required to increase the EU's absorption capacity. If this vision contains Treaty change, Berlin will need to find like-minded Member States to push for the respective measures which will launch this procedure. Scholz' speech in Prague during August 2022 merely outlined the general framework of reform proposals. However, the January 2023 French-German declaration put forward a more detailed agenda referring to decision-making, preservation of the rule of law and increasing democracy in the EU.

Thirdly, the EU's enlargement policy itself needs reform and the current circumstances certainly open a window of opportunity for this. All sides involved—the EU, the Member States and the candidate countries—need to be open to the concept of differentiation within the accession process. While not giving up on any requirements of strict conditionality and deepening of the EU, Germany's support for enlargement does though require a less rigid position which is open to the idea of a more differentiated approach to the EU's accession procedure. Differentiation should clearly be merit-based and allow for multi-speed accession instead of permanently excluding candidate countries.

Funda Tekin , Ph.D., is Director at Institut für Europäische Politik (IEP), External Senior Research Fellow at the Centre of Turkey and European Union Studies (CETEUS), University of Cologne, Honorary Professor at University Tübingen and board member of TEPSA.

Since its founding in1959, IEP has been a non-profit organisation dedicated to the study of European integration. It is one of the leading foreign and European policy research centres in Germany, serving as a forum for exchange between academia, politics, administration and political education. IEP's mission is to apply scholarly research to issues of European politics and integration, propose ways forward and promote the practical implementation of its research findings. IEP is also a member of TEPSA.

Greece, EU Enlargement and the 'Thessaloniki Promise'

Daniel Furby and Dimitris Tsaknis

On 10 June 2022, Politico carried an article by Greek Prime Minister Kyriakos Mitsotakis entitled, 'It's time to get European enlargement back on track'. This article was aimed to coincide with the South-East European Cooperation Process Summit then taking place under Greece's Presidency. Its appearance in Politico was also a clear indication that its target audience was European rather than domestic. Against a backdrop of Russia's invasion of Ukraine and ahead of the June European Council on 'Wider Europe', Ukraine and enlargement, Mitsotakis sought to establish a strong geo-strategic case for renewing the European Union's (EU) enlargement agenda, with a particular emphasis on the Western Balkans. Mitsotakis recalled the June 2003 European Council gathering in the Greek port city of Thessaloniki, which had 'offered a political vision of belonging and proposed a process that would lead to the Western Balkans' membership in the European family'. Why had the enlargement agenda subsequently stalled? Mitsotakis appeared to attribute primary responsibility to the EU itself: 'in the almost 20 years that have passed (since the Thessaloniki European Council), accession processes have increasingly become more elaborate and demanding, and the vision has become blurry, fading in the eyes of frustrated and disillusioned citizens'. The article proposed an ambitious new target of 2033 for the countries of the Western Balkans to join the EU. 'It is time', Mitsotakis concluded, 'to keep our Thessaloniki promise'.

The consistent support that Greece has shown for EU enlargement to the Western Balkans, across two decades, should be understood as part of a strategic approach to the future of South-Eastern Europe more generally. History and geography ensure that order and stability in the Western Balkans is of much more immediate concern to Athens than it might be to other, less geographically proximate capitals. That conflict in the region is a relatively recent memory could be seen as a reason for caution. From the Greek government's perspective, though, it provides an explicit

---

D. Furby (✉) · D. Tsaknis
European Public Law Organization, Athens, Greece
e-mail: dfurby@elgs.eu; dtsaknis@eplo.int

justification for further EU enlargement. Greek support for the Western Balkan countries' EU membership aspirations also has the potential to yield dividends through the settlement of bilateral disagreements in ways satisfactory to Greek policy-makers (if not always to Greek public opinion). The 2018 Prespa agreement between Greece and North Macedonia (previously known as the Republic of Macedonia) affords perhaps the clearest example of the nexus between Greece's support for the Euro-Atlantic integration of the Western Balkans, the promotion of regional order and stability, as well as the resolution of bilateral disputes.

The Erdogan Factor

Another key factor in Greece's strategic approach to South-Eastern Europe, including EU enlargement, is also its dominant foreign policy concern: namely, Recep Erdogan's Türkiye. Tensions between Greece and Türkiye have a long history, but today centre on competing claims in the Aegean and Eastern Mediterranean—particularly as regards exclusive economic zones, the sovereignty of certain Greek islands and energy resources. Confronted with increasingly hostile rhetoric from the Turkish President, including warnings that Turkish forces may arrive 'suddenly one night', Greece has sought to strengthen its defence capabilities in the Aegean. There is also a perception, and not a little frustration, among Greek policy-makers that other EU Member States do not take due account of Türkiye's hostile posture towards Greece in the context of their own bilateral relations with Ankara.

Greek concern about the potential for Türkiye to be a destabilising influence in the Western Balkans—for example, through its relations with Albania and Kosovo—and thereby to threaten Greek security, is an important element in the Greek case for enlargement. Mitsotakis' Politico article referred ominously to 'hostile actors seeking to undermine our efforts. They have a competing world view and aspirations that trample over human rights, the rule of law and fundamental freedoms. They use the language of resentment, revisionism and imperial nostalgia'. Against the background of war in Ukraine, many readers would probably have interpreted this as a reference to Putin's Russia. It is equally likely, though, that Mitsotakis had in mind Erdogan's Türkiye.

An Elite Consensus

The Greek approach to EU enlargement is underpinned by a broad consensus among its major political parties (New Democracy, PASOK, and SYRIZA), which in turn reflects the strong strategic and security concerns that underpin this policy. SYRIZA, which had been expected to challenge New Democracy for power in the May 2023 General Election, but ultimately finished a distant second, supports enlargement to the Western Balkans while recognising the need for reforms to address issues such as corruption and minority rights. The main reservation to be encountered at the level of elite opinion concerns Albania's candidacy. In that specific case, Greek minority rights is one among various issues that are regularly mentioned.

Consensus among political elites/parties, though, is not matched by equivalent support for enlargement at the level of public opinion. Eurobarometer polls indicate that Greek public attitudes towards widening EU membership have fluctuated over time and may also vary according to the prospective Member State. A recent increase in public support for enlargement means that in summer 2022, 55% of Greeks reported being in favour of enlargement (slightly below the EU average of 57%), while 36% said they were against. This improvement came after a decline in public enthusiasm for enlargement between the mid-2000s and mid-2010s, which may have reflected increased mistrust of EU institutions during the eurozone crisis. That prior decline, alongside bilateral tensions with certain Western Balkans countries (notably Albania and North Macedonia), may help to explain why—despite strong elite level support—public enthusiasm for enlargement in Greece remains below the EU average.

From Promise to Progress: Strengthening the Enlargement Agenda

Any assessment of Greece's approach to EU enlargement must inevitably address the question: why does the 'Thessaloniki promise' remain unfulfilled and what changes would be needed to deliver improved results in future? In his Politico article, Mitsotakis referred to increasing demands on applicant/candidate countries and a blurring of the enlargement 'vision'. Yet, there are few signs that the Greek government itself has a clear vision on how the many obstacles to EU enlargement can be overcome. This is perhaps unsurprising given the range of challenges faced by Greece since the 2008/2009 financial crisis. However, with the EU's renewed emphasis on enlargement following Russia's invasion of Ukraine, there is an opportunity for the country to work with like-minded Member States in order to ensure that the topic remains high on the list of EU priorities. Equally, it is necessary to address the uncertainties and tensions in the EU's approach to enlargement over the past decade and a half.

Particular consideration should be given to: (1) the need for stronger political leadership of the enlargement dossier within EU institutions; and (2) potential changes to EU enlargement methodology in order to provide a greater balance between 'conditionality' and incentives for applicant/candidate countries to implement necessary reforms.

Strong political leadership at the level of EU institutions is essential to guard against the possibility (perhaps the certainty) that Member States will lose focus on enlargement as other problems and crises arise. More specifically, it is vital that the next European Commission (to be appointed in 2024) should make progress towards enlargement a priority for the next 5 years. That would mean inter alia elevating the enlargement Commissioner's status relative to other portfolios within the College. Alternatively, and as has been suggested elsewhere, the Commission President could appoint a prominent figure from outside the College. In the case of Brexit, for example (often described as 'enlargement in reverse'), Michel Barnier was appointed as Head of the Article 50 Task Force and EU chief negotiator. Barnier was also invited to update the European Council on the United Kingdom's withdrawal negotiations and thereby ensured that EU heads of government regularly discussed the topic and were aware of the major risks and challenges.

While Mitsotakis' Politico article complained about 'elaborate and demanding' accession processes, the Greek government does not appear to hold very precise views on what a more appropriate level of conditionality would be—namely, which reforms are a necessary precursor to EU membership and where a less stringent stance might be possible. Rather than reducing conditionality per se (which is unlikely to be acceptable to more enlargement 'sceptical' countries), a more promising approach might be to strengthen incentives for reform, for example by making certain benefits of EU membership available to candidate countries as part of a phased approach to EU accession. Participation in the Single Market, as a step towards full EU membership, could be one such possibility.

With the appointment of a new Commission on the horizon, now is the moment for Greece and other pro-enlargement Member States to propose ambitious steps of this kind, which can help to ensure that the 'Thessaloniki promise' is finally kept.

Daniel Furby , Ph.D., is a Lecturer at the European Law and Governance School, International University School of the European Public Law Organization (EPLO), in Athens. He previously taught at Queen Mary, University of London, where he completed his doctorate on the United Kingdom's entry to the European Community. His research has also focused on Brexit and the process by which an independent Scotland might seek to join the EU.

Dimitris Tsaknis is a Research Associate at the European Public Law Organization (EPLO). He holds a Master's degree in International Relations from the National and Kapodistrian University of Athens. His research focuses primarily on European defence questions, terrorism and the Middle East.

EPLO is an international organisation, based in Athens, dedicated to the creation and dissemination of knowledge in the area of Public Law lato sensu and Governance. 17 countries have already ratified the International Treaty establishing EPLO.

Enlargement at All Costs? A View from Hungary

Veronika Czina, Tamás Szigetvári, and Gábor Túry

Generally Pro-Enlargement Stance

The current Hungarian foreign policy is committed to the integration of the Western Balkan countries and has been supportive in this regard ever since the country first gained European Union (EU) Membership in 2004. Hungary borders the Western Balkans and hence the region's stability is crucial in both political and economic senses. However, compared to its previous strategy, the EU is now more cautious, preferring a stricter conditionality and slower accession for (potential) candidate countries. By contrast, Hungary is keen to speed up enlargement and would not only want to accelerate the process, but would also prefer to ease accession conditions. Nevertheless, it is recognised that rapid enlargement could undermine the entire European integration project's internal cohesion and thus do more harm than good.

Based on the June/July 2022 Eurobarometer survey among the population, the proportion of those who support enlargement in Hungary is far higher (70%) than the EU average (57%), but in the middle range regarding those who are against (25%). Amongst neighbouring countries, such as Austria, Slovakia and Croatia, support for enlargement is much lower.

Political Motivation

The reason behind this current Hungarian pro-enlargement strategy is the dominant government party's (Fidesz) search for a foreign policy alliance. Hungarian foreign policy, which serves the interests of Fidesz, maintains close relations not with countries, but with parties. The Hungarian Prime Minister, Viktor Orbán has friendly relations with former Macedonian Prime Minister Nikola Gruevski and current

---

V. Czina (✉) · T. Szigetvári · G. Túry
Institute of World Economics, Centre for Economics and Regional Studies, Budapest, Hungary
e-mail: czina.veronika@krtk.hu; szigetvari.tamas@krtk.hu; tury.gabor@krtk.hu

© The Author(s), under exclusive license to Springer Nature Switzerland AG 2023
M. Kaeding et al. (eds.), *Enlargement and the Future of Europe*,
https://doi.org/10.1007/978-3-031-43234-7_13

Serbian Prime Minister Aleksandar Vučić. Moreover, having more countries of a similar size in the EU, not to mention the increasing weight of Eastern European countries in the integration process would certainly be beneficial for Hungary, by strengthening its block-building ability and regional position. Péter Szijjártó, Hungary's Minister of Foreign Affairs and Trade reaffirmed this position in March 2023 at the Budapest Balkans Forum. He emphasised that for Hungary enlargement is a matter of national security, because immigration can be handled only with effective cooperation from the Western Balkan countries. He also added that the EU is in a very bad shape, partly due to the failure of its enlargement policy and that those opposed to enlargement weaken the EU itself.

Whilst supporting the accession of all Western Balkan countries generally, Hungary shows a special interest towards Serbia. Speaking in Tirana during December 2022, Prime Minister Orbán argued that enlargement towards the Balkans is a vital issue in terms of Hungary's security, because the migration route can be closed permanently only with Serbia's help. He also emphasised that Western Balkan countries' EU accession is also a key issue from the perspective of energy security, since today Hungary's only supply route for natural gas is by means of the Southern corridor, namely through the Balkans via Serbia.

The Hungarian Enlargement Commissioner Olivér Várhelyi is sometimes accused of being lenient towards the Serbian leadership and having too favourable an opinion of Serbia which calls the impartial nature of his office into question. Many see this as part of efforts aimed at strengthening Hungary's position in the Western Balkans, so that following enlargement, Hungary will be able to bring allied Member States to its side in order to strengthen its own position. These potential allies would be countries where there are serious problems with the rule of law, freedom of the press or the transparency and cleanliness of public procurement.

Even though Budapest emphasises preservation of the Dayton Agreement creating the current form of Bosnia and Herzegovina, it has strongly sided with Serbian separatist aspirations in Bosnia. Apart from Belgrade, the Republika Srpska and its autocratic leader Milorad Dodik now have only Putin and the Hungarian government as foreign allies.

Concerning the Hungarian stance on Ukraine's membership perspectives, Orbán criticised the EU for letting itself 'drift into the war' due to sanctions and providing training and arms for Ukraine. He maintains that Hungary is in favour of Ukraine's EU Membership, certainly wants peace, but does not support any further sanctions against Russia. The generally supportive Hungarian stance towards further Eastern enlargement of the EU (with Moldova and even Georgia) has of late become more cautious, in view of the sharpening geopolitical context.

The Effect of Other Actors

Russian and Chinese influence is present in the Western Balkan region, with investment and loans as well as infrastructure developments and defence strategies. Hungary's particularist strategy strengthens the growing influence of Russia and

China in the region. Examples include: Chinese and Russian vaccine purchases during COVID-19; Hungary's attitude towards sanctions against Russia; and the Budapest-Belgrade railway line, which is financed by China. A common point in the strategy of Hungarian and some Western Balkan politicians is that they use their tight political and economic cooperation with third countries as a bargaining chip in their relations with Brussels. Orbán claims that contact with Russia and economic links with China are essential if Europe is to remain competitive.

Hurdles Within the EU's Democratic Functioning

The EU has faced significant challenges regarding decision-making over recent years. Hungary has used its veto on various occasions for votes requiring a unanimous decision in the European Council. For the first time in 2020, together with Poland, Hungary also put this veto into perspective when the 2021–2027 Multiannual Financial Framework was being adopted. Although the country voted for all economic sanctions against Russia in 2022, it vetoed certain political sanctions. It is not without precedent in the EU that a State has used a veto with its own interests in mind, but it was only in the case of Hungary that the adoption of a joint EU declaration was blocked because it represented the interests of a third country (Russia).

Concerning further EU enlargement, though, Hungary' government is among the most active supporters, never blocking or slowing down this process. Regarding the national minority policy of Ukraine, which raised severe criticism from Budapest, the Hungarian blocking potential was used for Ukraine's NATO rather than EU accession.

Recommendations

The key to efficient enlargement policy cooperation is to have unchanging requirements and a consistent monitoring system. The EU should enlarge, but only if this is in line with its post-accession monitoring mechanism. Reforms in (potential) EU candidate countries should be undertaken on a bottom-up basis: administrative capacity building is very important because no money can be well-spent if distribution systems are inefficient. Enlargement should not only imply geopolitical expansion, but military interventions could also be included in the EU's future toolbox, albeit not in the context of enlargement.

According to Péter Balázs, former Commissioner for Hungary, the situation in Ukraine derails the EU's previous enlargement philosophy, creates new political challenges for the EU, but can also bring forward new solutions. Slowing down the accession process can only lead to a kind of fatigue in candidate countries. The political and social acceptance of integration may decrease which may force change in that current candidate countries may not have to go through the same acquis communautaire adoption as countries that joined in the 1990s and 2000s. There are countries that are brought closer to accession only on political grounds (see Ukraine and Moldova).

This will most probably lead to a multi-speed enlargement system in Europe. Such a change could go both ways: it could freshen up the enlargement policy in its entirety, or it could undermine its basic principles. The multi-speed approach could be a preferable scenario for Hungary—at least under the current political leadership—because it would provide a precedent for opt-outs and a certain kind of half-speed EU Membership. Should this multi-speed enlargement system prevail, the EU should consider whether this kind of membership could also be available for old Member States (will there be a step back from their membership status), or only for new additions? This danger exists, which unfortunately creates a precedent for the legitimacy of Member States leaving the Economic and Monetary Union, in other words a two-speed Europe.

Enlargement Commissioner Olivér Várhelyi claims that times are changing, in the sense that Europe could also position itself as offering rather than always demanding a policy which could produce better results. Concerning Hungary's standpoint on EU enlargement, instead of rapid enlargement, the Hungarian government should support policies that strengthen the internal cohesion of the EU. It is necessary, inter alia, to reform decision-making in order to make efficient and quick responses to external and internal challenges and this could be done only by ending the requirement of unanimity. The 'more the merrier' enlargement philosophy pushed by Hungary's government could be dangerous and should at least for now be avoided considering the current critical circumstances being faced in the EU neighbourhood.

Veronika Czina Ph.D., is a Research Fellow at the HUN-REN CERS, Institute of World Economics. She holds a master's degree in international relations from the Eötvös Loránd University (2012) and from Central European University (2013). She earned her Ph.D. in Legal Studies from the University of Debrecen in 2021. In recent years, she has been teaching as an External Lecturer at Eötvös Loránd University, Institute of Political and International Studies. Her research focuses on Hungary's EU membership, EU integration and policy-making.

Tamás Szigetvári Ph.D., Habil., is an Associate Professor and Head of the International Studies Department at the Institute of International Studies and Political Sciences of the Pázmány Péter Catholic University, Budapest. He is also a Senior Research Fellow at the HUN-REN CERS, Institute of World Economics. He earned his MSc in Economics from the Budapest University of Economic Studies (today Corvinus University of Budapest) in 1996, and his Ph.D. in International Relations in 2003 from the same university.

Gábor Túry Ph.D., is a Research Fellow at the HUN-REN CERS, Institute of World Economics (since 2001). He holds a master's degree in geography from the Eötvös Loránd University (2001) and a PhD from social geography (2015). Since 2012, he has been teaching at the Pázmány Péter Catholic University, Eötvös Loránd University and the Budapest Business School.

The Centre for Economic and Regional Studies, Institute of World Economics analyses world economic processes and their impact on Hungary. It is the oldest and thereby most experienced Hungarian institute in this regard. Its primary goal is to draw on a local tradition of research and thus contribute to the international scientific sphere through exploratory research and valuable contributions in service of a common good and a brighter future.

Further Enlargement of the European Union: The View from Dublin

John O'Brennan

On 1 January 2023, Ireland reached a historic milestone, namely the 50th anniversary of its European Union (EU) membership, which also constituted the 50th anniversary of the Union's first enlargement. In many ways, Ireland might be viewed as the most successful candidate state to join the EU from previous rounds of accession. It has used its membership as a vehicle to launch a hugely ambitious programme covering the national development and modernisation of its economy and society. In the process it transformed itself from the poorest of the nine Member States in 1973 to amongst the richest of the 27 in 2023. Indeed, such has been the scale of transformation that Ireland is frequently cited by candidate states as a model of EU success. Thus, it seemed appropriate to many that the historic formal celebration of the 2004 accessions happened under an Irish EU Presidency in 2004. That day was named the 'Day of Welcomes' and included a formal ceremony in Dublin as well as street events all around Ireland which paired new Member States with specific Irish cities and towns.

Ireland has been consistently supportive of EU enlargement from the earliest days of its membership. Throughout the protracted accession process in the Western Balkans and more recently the 'Eastern partnership' region, where a subset of EU Member States has been consistently obstructive in regard to further accessions, Ireland has been continually and substantively supportive of the candidates. In late 2022 a public opinion poll conducted by polling company Red C demonstrated that 62% of the Irish people agree with a proposition that the EU 'should continue to allow more countries to join'. Moreover, 65% were also in favour of Ukraine joining the Union.

Perhaps the most important reason why there is such consistent support for further enlargement is the perception amongst policy-makers that, as a once poor, peripheral state which has benefitted enormously from membership of the EU, Ireland should

---

J. O'Brennan (✉)
Maynooth University, Maynooth, Ireland
e-mail: john.obrennan@mu.ie

© The Author(s), under exclusive license to Springer Nature Switzerland AG 2023
M. Kaeding et al. (eds.), *Enlargement and the Future of Europe*,
https://doi.org/10.1007/978-3-031-43234-7_14

not stand in the way of other European states that wish to participate in the European integration process, utilising it to enhance their development and convergence with EU norms.

Ireland's demography has changed significantly over the last quarter of a century. Along with Sweden and the United Kingdom, Ireland was one of just three Member States to open its labour markets to nationals from the 2004 entrants immediately. Ireland is now home to an estimated 120,000 Poles, 100,000 Romanians, 40,000 Lithuanians and 25,000 Croatians. Moreover, in response to the Russian invasion of Ukraine in 2022, Ireland has accepted and settled more than 75,000 Ukrainian refugees, a significantly higher proportion per head of population than most Member States. There is significant evidence to confirm that these EU nationals have been successfully integrated into Ireland's workforce and society. The experience of managing large-scale inward migration effectively associated with different phases of EU enlargement has created a virtuous cycle of support for further enlargement. In part, this is because of new transport connections from Ireland to all 27 Member States and many of the candidate states. Ireland is the only Member State to have an embassy in every other Member State of the EU.

Because the Irish economy is home to most of the world's leading multinational companies in sectors such as biopharma, information communication technologies and medical technology, it has become one of the most important vectors of globalisation in Europe. Ireland's attitude to the world beyond Irish shores is one of tolerance and inclusivity, regularly ranking in the annual KOF Globalisation index's top three countries. Within the EU, Ireland has championed policies that are pro-competition, pro-free trade and openness. It is aligned through the 'Hansa Group' with similar minded States such as Denmark, Estonia, Finland, Latvia, Lithuania, Netherlands and Sweden. While some of this subset of States has been very sceptical about the benefits of further enlargement (the Netherlands for example), Ireland has continued to champion the Western Balkans' cause (and more recently that of Ukraine). Ireland has been a net contributor to the EU since 2014. The change in status from net recipient to net contributor has had no appreciable impact on Irish attitudes to the EU or to further enlargement. If anything, support for both the EU and further enlargement has increased over the last decade.

Taoiseach (Prime Minister), Leo Varadkar, has repeatedly stressed a need for the EU to support economic convergence of Central and East European Member States as well as Western Balkan candidates via increases in structural funding. As a net contributor Ireland is not only willing to pay more, but can also point to its own history within the EU as proof that convergence via regional distribution really works. Support for further enlargement is shared across the party-political spectrum in Dublin, with very few dissenting voices in the Oireachtas (Parliament).

Recommendations

Firstly, Ireland is the only EU27 Member State with an embassy in every other Member State of the Union. Diplomatic relations with accession candidates are, though, still patchy. Hence, Ireland should commit to opening new embassies in Albania, Bosnia and Hercegovina, Georgia, Kosovo, Moldova, Montenegro, North Macedonia and Serbia, as soon as possible.

Secondly, 2023 sees not just the 50th anniversary of Ireland's EU membership, but also the 30th anniversary of the Good Friday Agreement. Ireland has a special sensitivity towards ethnic conflict and how peace agreements cannot only be secured, but also maintained. Irish nationals have vast experience of contributing to peace settlements in Bosnia, Kosovo and elsewhere. Thus, Ireland should offer itself as the key EU interlocutor between Kosovo and Serbia as well as between the constituent units of Bosnia and Herzegovina, with the aim of bringing that unique Irish sensitivity of contested identities and territory to help resolve the difficulties between candidate states.

Thirdly, Ireland offers an extraordinary example of how small States can use EU membership to transform their economies and societies. More specifically, it has attracted a disproportionately large share of foreign direct investments coming into the EU over the past 30 years. The Irish government should do more to share with candidate states the practices employed to help locate significant foreign direct investments in crucial sectors of the economy. This should include secondment of individuals from State agencies such as the Irish Development Authority, Enterprise Ireland and the Irish Food Board to equivalent agencies within the candidate countries.

Fourthly, Ireland should continue to support the European Commission's enlargement strategy and increase its financial contribution to the Western Balkans, Ukraine, Moldova and Georgia.

John O'Brennan, Ph.D., is a professor of European Politics in the Department of Sociology at Maynooth University, Ireland. He also holds the Jean Monnet Chair of European Integration at Maynooth and is Director of the Maynooth Centre for European and Eurasian Studies. He is widely published on EU Enlargement policy including the 2006 book, *The Eastern Enlargement of the European Union* (Routledge).

Maynooth University is Ireland's fastest-growing university, which celebrated its 25th birthday on 16 June 2022, having been formally established as an autonomous university in 1997. Yet, its origins can be traced back to the Royal College of St. Patrick's founding in 1795, drawing inspiration from a heritage that includes over 200 years of education and scholarship. Today, Maynooth University is a place of lively contrasts—a modern institution, dynamic, rapidly-growing, research-led and engaged, yet grounded in historic academic strengths and scholarly traditions.

Beyond 'Enlargement Fatigue': A View from Rome

Matteo Bonomi

There is a widespread misperception related to European Union (EU) 'enlargement fatigue' that associates the continuous stalemates in the formal process of EU enlargement with an effective suspension of third countries' integration into the Union. However, this does not fully correspond to reality.

On the contrary, the integration of enlargement countries has continued in its substance. If one looks at the EU candidate and potential candidate countries in the Western Balkans, for instance, they are much more integrated with the EU today than they were 10 years ago. This applies to all sectors of their economies, including goods, services, investments, finance and labour force, but it goes far beyond the integration of markets. This is true for many other fields, especially those sectors that have been affected by the multiple crises over recent years. These sectors have required much greater policy coordination, including the coordination of austerity policy, control of irregular migration, health issues and energy efficiency. In other words, beyond the formal EU enlargement policy framework, policy coordination has become the rule, not the exception and has driven EU integration during these difficult years.

Against this backdrop, the war in Ukraine and the ensuing opening of an EU accession perspective for three countries within the European Eastern Neighbourhood, coupled with the decision of granting candidate status to Ukraine and Moldova in particular, have triggered strong demands across Europe for full EU membership and have provided new impetus to the EU enlargement policy. As a result, enlargement, as a formal process of accession to the Union, seems to be back on track. In such a context, though, the central issue is how to maintain the momentum and make this new process of EU accession work in the long run, beyond the clear limits of current enlargement policy.

For governments that have traditionally been strong supporters of EU enlargement, such as those in Italy, this means that continuing simply to be in favour of

---

M. Bonomi (✉)
Istituto Affari Internazionali, Rome, Italy
e-mail: m.bonomi@iai.it

© The Author(s), under exclusive license to Springer Nature Switzerland AG 2023
M. Kaeding et al. (eds.), *Enlargement and the Future of Europe*,
https://doi.org/10.1007/978-3-031-43234-7_15

enlargement within the European Council while enhancing policy cooperation on the ground risks not being enough. Italy, together with the other Member States that are ready to support this process, should work proactively on a new political agenda for enlargement, which should aim not only at reinvigorating the EU's transformative power, but also contributing to the consolidation of a new Europe beyond the fatigue of enlargement.

From Fatigue to Ambiguity?

The EU's enlargement policy appears today to be populated by variegated practices of external cooperation, which present an exceptional, probably unique, degree of intensity and take place in an unprecedented number of policy areas. Building on the pre-accession framework and through new governance practices that are often informal and predominantly intergovernmental in nature, the EU has developed models of differentiated external cooperation aimed at transferring its practices and policies to actual as well as potential candidate countries for EU accession.

Seen from Rome, such circumstances have brought about another confirmation. Despite rising Euroscepticism and emerging enlargement fatigue in the country, integration between Italy and the Western Balkans has continued and deepened further. Indeed, during the recent crises, the Italian public has mostly turned against the accession of new members in the EU. Significantly, the (relative) majority of Italians had been constantly against further enlargements from autumn 2008 to summer 2020 according to the Eurobarometer. Yet, Italian elites and governments have consistently pursued a European agenda for countries in the Balkans.

This has been realised through increasing economic integration; for instance, trade in goods between Italy and the Western Balkan countries has doubled since 2010. However, increasing integration has taken place especially by enhancing policy coordination on the ground, from home and justice affairs to connectivity development and energy as well as digital transitions. This has been realised thanks to many formats that allow cooperation between governments and their agencies in more or less formalised ways (such as EUROPOL, FRONTEX, the Berlin Process, Connectivity Agenda, Western Balkan Investment Framework) and by maintaining the 'Stabilisation and Association Process' as an overarching strategy towards the region.

Thus, this type of integration appears very different from textbook definitions in the context of European integration history. There are at least three differences. Firstly, this is not taking place through laws (the so-called Integration Through Law), but predominantly through forms of coordination of national policies and intergovernmental cooperation, albeit adoption of the EU acquis has proceeded extremely slowly. Secondly, it is not having a teleological focus on accession to the EU but driven primarily by a pragmatic spirit and aimed at the need to find immediate answers to the challenges posed by interdependence. Finally, coordination is taking place above all in those areas affected by recent crises and thus not traditionally associated with EU integration, such as security and the use of coercive force, public finance and public administration (the so-called core state powers).

In other words, of late losing immediate prospects for membership has been matched by a substantial reorientation of the EU's enlargement policy towards a less teleological framework which, instead of aiming at full Union membership, is more open and pragmatic, aimed at fostering cooperation in a large number of key areas.

Limits of Current EU Enlargement Policy

The repetition of such a scheme in the EU enlargement policy of the future, beyond the current moment of intra-EU cohesion and agreement, clearly cannot be excluded. This form of integration for the Western Balkans provided pragmatic solutions to Member States' shift in preferences, the ensuing failure to meet a functional demand for greater integration and the scarcity of any political offer for it due to scepticism towards the entry of new members in some European capitals. Yet, one should also be mindful of the important limits within an integration process through policy coordination, which are particularly evident in the Western Balkans case.

Indeed, this type of integration with the Western Balkan countries has proved to be ineffective for various reasons. It has not stimulated an efficient distribution of resources and hence has not adequately sustained a process of economic convergence for these countries with the rest of Europe. Furthermore, it has failed to foster democratisation, as it has reinforced the national executive's role and power *vis-à-vis* all other domestic actors—something particularly problematic in the context of fragile democracies such as the Balkan states. Finally, it has proved illegitimate to the extent that it has placed the region's countries on a level of inequality with respect to neighbouring countries already belonging to the Union. On the one hand, this has favoured the interference of third parties in the region's affairs, as is well illustrated by the case of Chinese mask diplomacy that profited from the EU's initial hesitations to make the Western Balkans part of the European response to the pandemic. On the other hand, it has allowed for an incorrect use of the EU framework by Member States themselves. The latter have often imposed their preferences on candidate countries improperly, as most recently Bulgaria did regarding North Macedonia's adoption of the EU's negotiating framework.

Beyond Enlargement Fatigue

Accordingly, the opening of an accession perspective for Georgia, Moldova and Ukraine represents good news for all enlargement countries, since it testifies not simply a new momentum for EU enlargement, but the fact that enlargement policy might be back on track as a formal process for EU accession. It is no coincidence that the offer of candidate status to Ukraine and Moldova in June 2022 has been followed by the opening of accession negotiations with Albania and North Macedonia as well as the unanimous decision by EU leaders to grant EU candidate status to Bosnia and Herzegovina on 15 December 2022. In less than 6 months, the European Council has not only affirmatively replied to third countries demands of integration but has also supplied EU enlargement policy with positive decisions in a way that is unprecedented in recent European history. Moreover, these decisions by the Council have been accompanied by increasing support for EU enlargement among the general public in Italy as well as across Europe.

Nevertheless, one cannot expect that current conditions, which seem particularly favourable for EU enlargement, will last indefinitely. Those governments such as Italy's that support EU enlargement as a strategic objective of the Union should use this window of opportunity in which Member States seem ready to supply more integration in order to reinforce the EU enlargement agenda and transformative power.

Recommendations

To this end, the current limits of the EU enlargement policy towards the Western Balkans offer a guide for action. Italy, together with other Member States that are ready to support this process, should even before accession make efforts to provide the enlargement countries with additional supporting measures. These might include: (1) granting candidate countries with additional access to the EU budget even before accession, in order to strengthen economic convergence—for instance, through gradual access to EU cohesion funds; (2) bringing candidate countries closer to EU decision-making structures, in order to promote their institutional participation and citizens' involvement—for instance, including them as observers in some EU institutions; and (3) finding ways to limit abuse of the enlargement process by individual Member States for bilateral issues or other domestic problems—for instance, by exerting peer pressure within the European Council, or by considering a change in decision-making procedures.

In such a dynamic context, the Italian government cannot simply be satisfied by continuing to support EU enlargement in the European Council while enhancing policy cooperation on the ground. Italy has the necessary experience and weight to play a prominent role in contributing to reform of the enlargement policy, by putting it back on a more effective, sustainable and legitimate track.

Matteo Bonomi , Ph.D., is Senior Fellow in the 'EU, politics and institutions' programme at Istituto Affari Internazionali (IAI). His work focuses on European integration and EU enlargement policy. He has published academic and policy papers on various aspects of EU differentiated integration, Western Balkan-EU relations and the political economy of EU enlargement. He is member of the 'Balkans in Europe Policy Advisory Group' (BiEPAG).

IAI is a private, independent non-profit think tank, founded in 1965 on the initiative of Altiero Spinelli. It seeks to promote awareness of international politics and contribute to the advancement of European integration and multilateral cooperation. IAI is part of a vast international network and interacts and cooperates with national, European and international institutions, as well as with universities, major economic actors, the media and the most authoritative international think tanks.

Head and Heart in the Right Place: Latvia on the EU Enlargement

Aleksandra Palkova and Karlis Bukovskis

European Union (EU) enlargement has always been a complex and politically charged issue. Latvia's stance is not special in this regard. Balancing the logic of consequences with that of appropriateness, Latvia has always taken a cautious approach to the idea of EU enlargement and managed to align its national position with the common stance amongst many other Member States, namely: 'if everyone else runs, I will run too'. In other words, Latvia's perspective has been that if the European Commission and other EU Member States support the accession of a particular country, then Latvia will not prevent it.

Copenhagen Criteria as a Must

EU enlargement has naturally been the subject of much debate and concern among EU Member States. One key worry raised by many countries, including Latvia, is the impact of enlargement on the distribution of cohesion funds, which are a crucial source of financing for the EU's poorest regions, including Latvia. While Latvians were only slightly in favour of further EU enlargement following their country's own accession, the political elite did not want to be seen as hypocritical by stopping further enlargements immediately after Latvia itself had been accepted. Meanwhile, to address the population's fears that new accessions could result in less cohesion funding for Latvia, its position was tied to the condition of strict implementation of the Copenhagen Criteria. In this way, Latvia tried to ensure that new Member States would meet the necessary standards and hence would not challenge the EU's political stability and economic security. Even now, as Latvia is advocating for Ukraine's accession, the Copenhagen Criteria remain essential in the country's

A. Palkova · K. Bukovskis (✉)
Latvian Institute of International Affairs, Riga, Latvia
e-mail: aleksandra.palkova@liia.lv; karlis.bukovskis@liia.lv

reasoning and thus their strict implementation has always been a key component within the Latvian enlargement stance.

According to a Eurobarometer survey conducted in 2019, 56% of Latvians believe that EU enlargement has been good for their country, while only 12% believe it has been bad. The same survey also found that 54% of Latvians believe in future EU enlargement, while 22% are opposed. In terms of Latvian political parties, their views on enlargement vary, but all are generally supportive, for instance by expressing support for North Macedonia and Albania's accession to the EU in 2020 and more recently Ukraine, Moldova, and Georgia. The difference is seen in the parties individual MEPs' positions, with some expressing more caution about enlargement, voicing concerns about potential security and economic risks. However, the opposition parties are generally supportive, albeit certain individuals have also expressed concerns about enlargement, calling for stricter conditions for candidate countries and a stronger focus on EU integration for existing Member States, which before further enlargement should also receive active EU encouragement to concentrate on deepening integration. It should be noted, though, that these are general trends, given that individual politicians and parties may have differing views on specific enlargement issues and candidate countries.

Latvia's Shift in Approach to EU Enlargement

Latvia's position on EU enlargement became significantly more open following establishment of the Eastern Partnership (EaP) in 2009, which aimed at EU engagement with six countries in Eastern Europe through promotion of democracy, human rights and economic cooperation. Latvia saw this partnership as a way of advancing its own national interests and thus offered wholehearted support. The EaP provided opportunities for Latvia not only to strengthen its ties with Belarus, Moldova, Ukraine, Georgia, Armenia and Azerbaijan, but also to promote its economic interests. Additionally, the EaP provided a platform for Latvia to advance its regional political and security interests where it was important so as to balance Russia's presence in EaP countries.

A notable departure from Latvia's position on EU enlargement was demonstrated by its stance on Serbia's accession to the EU. This case demonstrated that Latvia was willing to use the enlargement process as political leverage in order to protect its own national and security interests, given Serbia's support towards Russia after its full-scale attack on Ukraine in 2022. Such friendly relations were certainly deemed unacceptable by Latvia. The Latvian Foreign Minister threatened to veto Serbia's accession negotiations and stated that 'EU candidate countries must adopt EU foreign policy guidelines and directions of action; if Serbia does not do so, especially in the context of Russia's invasion of Ukraine, then Latvia will not support further integration of Serbia into the EU and the negotiation process'. Latvia's unusually vocal position on the enlargement process was motivated by its desire to promote stability and security in Europe, thus counterbalancing Russia's influence elsewhere in the Balkan region.

It is evident that Latvia considers enlargement to be a crucial part of the EU's growth and development. In terms of priorities, the country has repeatedly emphasised the importance of maintaining a strong focus on the EU's programmes, which aim to support democratic reform and economic development amongst Eastern neighbours. Latvia has also emphasised the need for the EU to continue to support reforms and democratic progress in existing Member States, including addressing issues such as the rule of law and corruption. Latvia has always been broadly in favour of EU enlargement, with the inclusion of new countries being seen as a way of promoting stability and security in Europe, albeit under reasonable conditions. Increasingly vocal support for Ukraine's membership in the EU has become visible since mid-2022. Hence, when EU countries decide to 'jump' towards future enlargement, Latvia will follow.

Recommendations

In conclusion, Latvia's position on EU enlargement is shaped by its commitment to both the EU and its own national interests. While there was initial concerns about the impact on cohesion funds, the country has fully recognised that enlargement is a vital part of the EU's growth and development. Latvia is prepared to be supportive if it is in the best interests of the EU as a whole, in other words if most Member States vote for further enlargement. By balancing its commitment to EU enlargement with its own domestic perspectives, Latvia has managed to remain a trustworthy partner to countries that were members before 2004 and those that followed. The ease of future EU enlargements would be facilitated by:

Firstly, encouraging candidate countries to implement reforms: Latvia should continue to promote the implementation of necessary reforms amongst candidates to meet the EU's standards and values. This can be done through providing technical assistance and support to help address specific challenges and by engaging in dialogue to promote the benefits of EU Membership.

Secondly, addressing concerns about economic impact: Latvia should work with other EU Member States to alleviate worries about the potential economic impact of enlargement. This can be done by promoting policies that support economic growth and development in both existing and new Member States.

Thirdly, ensuring fair engagement and burden-sharing: Latvia should ensure that tasks and responsibilities of enlargement are shared fairly among EU Member States. This can be done by ensuring that all Member States contribute to the costs of enlargement and are being actively engaged in helping prospective candidate countries.

Aleksandra Palkova is a Researcher at the Latvian Institute of International Affairs and Political science Ph.D. student. She is a Senior Researcher at Riga Stradins University (RSU), where she studies security and climate policy issues. Since 2021 Palkova has been an Associate Researcher at the European Council on Foreign Relations (ECFR). Since 2022 Aleksandra Palkova has been a guest lecturer at Riga Stradins University and Vidzemes Augstskola.

Karlis Bukovskis, Ph.D., is the Director of the Latvian Institute of International Affairs and an Assistant Professor at Riga Stradins University. He is the author of numerous articles and the scientific editor of several books. Bukovskis was a visiting Fulbright Scholar at the Johns Hopkins University SAIS in 2021 and an Associate Researcher at the European Council on Foreign Relations from 2017–2021. Bukovskis also produces and co-hosts a programme on Latvian Radio 1 in which he analyses the political economy of various world countries. LIIA is the oldest Latvian think tank that specialises in foreign and security policy analysis. This independent research institute conducts research, develops publications and organises public lectures as well as conferences related to global affairs along with Latvia's international role and policies. The LIIA is also a member of TEPSA.

Lithuania's Strong Support for the EU's 'Open Door' Policy: How to Make Use of the Geopolitical Window of Opportunity

Ramūnas Vilpišauskas

Lithuania has been a consistent supporter of European Union (EU) enlargement since it joined the Union in 2004. However, until 2022 even granting the status of candidate countries to EU's Eastern neighbours—Lithuania's key priority—seemed very distant. By contrast, the challenge now is how to turn the current geopolitical crisis into the EU's renewal and achieve the goal of creating a united Europe, free and at peace.

Since becoming a Member, Lithuania has consistently supported the EU's 'open door' policy. Further enlargement has been related to extending the area of security and stability to the EU's Eastern neighbourhood. Hence, the subject of enlargement has often been discussed jointly with the EU's Eastern neighbourhood policies. For example, on the day of Lithuania's accession to the EU the Lithuanian Parliament adopted a resolution outlining the country's foreign policy priorities, which reflected broad political consensus and formed the basis for future government programmes. It formulated a vision of Lithuania as a regionally visible actor exerting tangible influence on the EU's neighbourhood policies and supporting its 'open door' policy based on the Copenhagen Criteria for those countries that express their intention to join the Union. This strategic support for EU enlargement directed practical efforts for Lithuania's developmental assistance to Eastern neighbours to support political, economic and institutional reforms which could bring their countries closer to the EU.

Although the key focus in terms of future enlargement was on Eastern neighbours such as Ukraine, Georgia and Moldova, Lithuania's political elites also supported granting an EU accession perspective and assisting integration for Western Balkan countries. Moreover, Lithuanians were very enthusiastic about Iceland's accession to the EU following its official application in 2009, afterg the global financial crisis. Political support for Iceland's EU Membership was seen mostly as an expression of

R. Vilpišauskas (✉)
Institute of International Relations and Political Science, Vilnius University, Vilnius, Lithuania
e-mail: ramunas.vilpisauskas@tspmi.vu.lt

gratitude for its being the first country to recognise officially the re-establishment of Lithuania's independence in the early 1990s. This was also in line with the prioritisation of Baltic-Nordic cooperation.

However, a few years later domestic politics in Iceland led to a halting of its accession to the EU. Hence Croatia's EU Membership 10 years ago, welcomed by Lithuania which assumed rotating Presidency of the Council of the EU in mid-2013, marks the last instance of EU enlargement. But even before that one could see the growing frustration among Lithuania's diplomats and foreign policy-makers regarding the EU's reluctance to proceed with integration of its Eastern neighbours, especially its unwillingness even to grant them candidate status.

There were a couple of reasons behind this frustration with the EU's failure to act strategically. Lithuania's own experience since the 1990s was that an EU accession perspective has provided continuity to countries' transition reforms. During his speech at the London School of Economics in early 2008 President Valdas Adamkus mentioned the EU's power 'to mobilise and drive transformation', arguing that through its integration and enlargement mechanisms the EU has helped to transform the entire Central European region. Thus, the promise of EU Membership has been seen as a potentially powerful incentive to motivate elites in Ukraine, Georgia and Moldova to proceed with reforms and reinforce the processes of their Europeanisation. Moreover, the promise of EU Membership was also seen as a geopolitical factor which could, together with the perspective of NATO membership, counterbalance the growing influence of Russia (and China) in those countries. However, there was a sense in Lithuania that for the EU, or rather some of its large Member States, partnership with an increasingly aggressive Russia was more important than support for extending freedom, peace and prosperity to the EU's neighbouring countries.

Nevertheless, Lithuania's policy-makers continued to support reforms in Ukraine, Georgia and Moldova and their prospective integration into the EU. This has been pursued by acting as their advocate in the EU in promoting the reduction of barriers to the movement of people, liberalising trade between those countries and the EU, integrating energy and transport networks as well as approximating legal norms. These diplomatic efforts were supplemented with Lithuania's bilateral financial and technical assistance provided to those Eastern neighbours. The success of reforms in countries such as Ukraine was seen as an important factor in facilitating the bottom-up process of democratisation and similar reforms in Russia and Belarus.

Hence, support for EU enlargement has been consistently articulated by Lithuania's elites, who justify this on historical and geopolitical grounds. Although this issue has not featured much in domestic debates, the country's population has been generally supportive, especially after the aggressive actions of Russia against Eastern neighbours, which mobilised society's attention and support for their EU Membership. For example, according to the Eurobarometer survey conducted in Summer 2022, as many as 81% of Lithuania's respondents indicated their support for EU enlargement—the highest level among all EU Member States (EU27 average of 57%). Furthermore, in a Eurobarometer survey on EU's response to Russia's war against Ukraine conducted in April 2022, 82% of respondents from Lithuania indicated their support for Ukraine joining the EU when it is ready (EU27 average of 71%).

From a Lithuanian perspective, Russia's large scale war of aggression against Ukraine in 2022 has finally provided a window of opportunity for the EU to reassess its enlargement policy. However, this renewed attention on enlargement also reinforces the challenges related to reforms not only within candidate countries, but also the EU itself. While Lithuania's policy-makers continue to refer to the importance of Copenhagen Criteria being met by candidate countries, the concept of conditionality has become more nuanced. Alignment of candidate countries' foreign and security policies with the EU's relevant policies, for example, on economic sanctions, has been stressed as an important precondition for their integration into the EU. Moreover, there has been an increase in awareness of how important it is for the rule of law to be observed by future (and current) Members in order to preserve the EU's cohesion. Finally, there is a growing tension between Lithuania's position taken with respect to the EU's institutional reforms and support for its enlargement. In recent years there has been a visible tendency among the country's policy-makers to resist institutional EU reforms and support the status quo—the position which will need to be reconsidered when the next round of EU enlargement approaches.

Recommendations

Lithuania's support for the EU's 'open door' policy in combination with the merit-based approach of integrating candidate countries is well justified on both moral and pragmatic grounds. To advance this priority after the EU decided to grant candidate country status to Ukraine and Moldova in 2022, Lithuania's diplomats and policy makers should continue to provide financial, technical and political support for reforms in candidate countries, relying on existing contacts and high levels of trust amongst Eastern partners as well as knowledge of EU norms and patterns of cooperation. While being sympathetic with the enormous challenges being faced by Ukraine, they should be supportive of consistent reforms aimed at establishing the institutions, rules and routine practices with respect to the rule of law and other democratic key principles which form the EU's basis. The re-establishment of Ukraine's territorial integrity and sovereignty is a precondition for its successful reconstruction aligned with integration into the EU. Accordingly, as much support as possible should be provided, both bilaterally and through the EU and other institutional formats.

Lithuania should advocate extending the suspension of barriers to trade between the EU and Ukraine, preferably until it joins the EU's Single Market. At the same time, financial and technical assistance to facilitate alignment of Ukrainian businesses with EU regulatory norms should be provided. The liberalisation of trade and movement of people should be accompanied by removal of barriers to free movement of capital in Ukraine, including transparent rules of competition enforced by independent regulatory bodies, market entry and exit and reforms in the areas such as land sales. Similar approaches of accelerating integration into the EU's Single Market should be applied to other candidate countries.

Finally, Lithuania's policy-makers should conduct a public debate on potential pros and cons of EU institutional and budgetary reforms with a view to the Union's effective functioning after the next round of its enlargement. It should be noted that a public survey undertaken in 2020 as an input into country's debate on the Future of Europe showed that significant majorities of respondents in Lithuania support giving a stronger role to the EU in the areas of foreign, security and defence policies, while at the same time attaching important roles to NATO and cooperation with the US.

The current Lithuanian government formed in late 2020 stated in its programme that Lithuania should aim to bring back EU enlargement into 'the real agenda of the Union', envisioning the goal of achieving a membership perspective for Moldova, Georgia and Ukraine by 2027 when Lithuania again assumes Rotating Presidency of the Council of the EU. After what happened in 2022, the challenge is to make enlargement a reality in a context which is rather different from the 1990s and 2000s.

Ramūnas Vilpišauskas, Ph.D., is Jean Monnet Chair (2020–2023) Professor at the Institute of International Relations and Political Science (IIRPS), in Vilnius University. From 2009 to 2019, he was Director of the Institute. In 2004–2009, he worked as Chief Economic Policy Advisor to the President of Lithuania, Valdas Adamkus. His main research interests include the political economy of European integration, together with policy analysis of public sector reforms and international political economy.

The IIRPS at Vilnius University is one of the most prominent social sciences institutions in Eastern Europe and the Baltic region. The Institute is an academic institution specialising in social and political sciences. IIRPS is also a member of TEPSA.

Luxembourg: Get Ready to Enlarge

Guido Lessing

This year, 2023, marks the 50th anniversary of the first enlargement. As in 1973, when Denmark, Ireland and the United Kingdom joined the then-European Economic Community, Luxembourg backed all ensuing waves of new entrants into the bloc. Despite its small size, the country has also succeeded in defending its own interests in a growing community of States. Furthermore, during the various rounds of enlargement, Luxembourg has: provided three Commission Presidents; secured the seat of a European capital; and recorded economic growth well above the Union average. Moreover, all its neighbours were founding Members of the European Communities in the 1950s and thankfully all historical conflicts about borders as well as national sovereignty have long been resolved. Political rifts on the grounds of ethnic allegiance and territorial claims seem to be part of daily business for politicians in the Western Balkans, but completely inconceivable in the Luxembourgish context. There are no neighbours contesting its existence or cultural idiosyncrasies. From Luxembourg's experience, it is a truism that shared sovereignty through a rules-based system is also politically and economically stabilising in the wider European context. In this respect, a future for the European Union (EU) and Europe as a space of geopolitical weight is unthinkable without further enlargement. Ever since the Soviet Union fell, successive NATO enlargement rounds were voted for only half-heartedly by certain Members of the Luxembourg Parliament, whereas successive waves of EU enlargement were unanimously welcomed.

G. Lessing (✉)
Luxembourg Centre for Contemporary and Digital History, Esch-sur-Alzette, Luxembourg
e-mail: guido.lessing@ext.uni.lu

War as a Game Changer

Of course, the more external pressure on the EU increases, the more urgent becomes the need for enlargement. Interference from Russia and China in the EU and its neighbourhood can no longer be ignored. The Russian invasion of Ukraine certainly functions as a trigger for change in the general attitude towards enlargement, with general public support having increased noticeably since February 2022 to the point where it has become the majority opinion in Luxembourg. The fact that approval rates have risen by more than 50% in the Grand-Duchy compared to the situation just before the Russian invasion of Ukraine shows that war is a game changer—there is a time before 24 February 2022 and a time after 24 February 2022. Scepticism about an overstretched, dysfunctional EU seems to have dwindled in the face of external threats. On this point, at least, decision-makers are in step with their voters.

Unsurprisingly, since June 2022, the enlargement process has gained momentum not only by granting candidate status to Ukraine, Moldova and Bosnia and Herzegovina, but also by offering the prospect of this status to Georgia—even if we know that their accession to the EU will be a longer-term consideration.

Stay Fair!

Regarding the Western Balkans, where the granting of candidate status has been much harder to reach, the long-standing Luxembourg Minister of Foreign Affairs, Jean Asselborn, insists on a clear, transparent conditionality for accession to the EU. For Asselborn, the ball is now clearly in the court of the candidate countries, particularly their willingness to combat corruption and follow a reform agenda. In November 2022, he conceded though in his annual statement on Foreign and European Policy that the way individual countries have for years blocked the opening of accession negotiations with North Macedonia has sadly undermined the EU's credibility. Greece and Bulgaria obstructing accession talks with their neighbour on the grounds of nationalist narratives has gone down badly in Luxembourg. Moreover, Luxembourg's existence as an independent country was itself repeatedly threatened on historic and cultural grounds by all its neighbours throughout the first half of the twentieth century. The Grand-Duchy also has a visible community of people from ex-Yugoslavia who fled the war-torn Western Balkans some 30 years ago. Geographically, the Western Balkan countries are not on the doorstep of Luxembourg, but they are perceived as belonging to the European house.

Pressure for Reform

A series of central questions arise from the perspective of further enlargements which becomes increasingly important in the face of external threats: how can the EU institutionally absorb new entrants and guarantee efficiency in its decision-making process? How can the EU avoid single Member countries preventing enlargement based on national agendas? How can the EU guarantee that democratic structures in new Member States are sustainable and that they will not dismantle the rule of law after accession? (Further cases of 'illiberal democracies' must be avoided.) Finally, how can the EU respond to potential frustrations in the applicant countries on their long and bumpy way to accession?

Financially, Ukraine's accession will be the EU's biggest challenge. In any case, once peace has returned the country needs to be rebuilt, which will hopefully be soon. Of course, the EU cannot shoulder such massive reconstruction responsibilities alone. The World Bank, the International Monetary Fund and the international community will all have to carry their share.

Institutionally, EU enlargement by many small Member States in the Western Balkans is much more challenging. If the EU does not want to be blocked by its own decision-finding processes, unanimity must end even in sensitive matters of Common Foreign and Security Policy, EU Membership and the identification of breaches in EU values. The dilemma is that with each new Member entering the EU, the hurdle of unanimity becomes more difficult to overcome. If the strongest instrument for change is the negotiation process for accession, the strongest instrument to paralyse the EU is Membership.

Although enhanced cooperation has the potential to attenuate still further the strong requirement of unanimity in some fields, logically this cannot be the case when it comes to enlargement. As it will be difficult to give up the principle of unanimity between Member States for the final decision on accession of new entrants, stronger involvement by the European Parliament in the run-up to candidates' accession would exert the necessary pressure on potential blockers.

Recommendations

Firstly, the European Parliament must be given the sole right to decide on the status of candidacy based on recommendations by the Commission. This would be more democratic and put pressure on reluctant Member States to vote in line with the majority.

Secondly, it is imperative that the Union's credibility is not compromised regarding accession requirements. At the same time, national legislatures of new Member States must share their experiences of the accession process with their peers in new candidate countries in a best practice approach.

Thirdly, to avoid further frustration in candidate countries on the long road to full Membership, the 'Norway' option—being a non-voting Member of the Single Market—would be a promising step. Participation in the Erasmus+ Programme, in security and even monetary cooperation as in Kosovo and Montenegro will give the process a new dynamic.

Fourthly, the terrain sketched out by the general regime of conditionality for protection of the Union's budget is also promising for future breaches in the principles of law, not just in Hungary, but throughout all Member States. The conditionality mechanism promises to have great leverage even in an EU with 30 Members and more. This instrument needs to be developed to protect the values of democracy and the rule of law.

Guido Lessing is a Research Assistant at the Luxembourg Centre for Contemporary and Digital History (University of Luxembourg). He has many years' experience teaching history and civics in secondary school and has also co-authored various history and civics textbooks. After working for the Centre d'Etudes et de Recherches Européennes Robert Schuman (CERE) in Luxembourg, he joined the C2DH in September 2017. His main fields of interest are European integration and the history of Luxembourg in the twentieth century.

C2DH is the University of Luxembourg's third interdisciplinary research centre, focusing on high-quality research, analysis and public dissemination in the field of contemporary Luxembourgish and European history. It promotes an interdisciplinary approach with a particular focus on new digital methods and tools for historical research and teaching.

Malta and Enlargement: Supportive But Not Engaged

Mark Harwood

Malta's somewhat tortuous journey to European Union (EU) membership took a long 17 years in all to complete. When the Christian Democrats were elected to government in 1987, they waited 3 years before applying in 1990 as many EU Member States were considered less than enthusiastic for this smallest of countries to join. Once the Commission published its opinion (*avis*) in 1993, it became clear that administrative capacity, economic openness and Malta's neutrality would be major issues that the country needed to address. However, by then the EU had become increasingly pre-occupied with its Eastern neighbours while the other Mediterranean applicants (Cyprus and Türkiye) placed Malta in an inauspicious group. With little progress in its application and a polarisation between Malta's two main parties (with the Christian Democrats in favour of joining and the Social Democrats opposed), Malta's application was frozen in 1996. This was reactivated in 1998 (after the Social Democrats were ousted from power after only 2 years), with the issue finally being resolved in the 2003 membership referendum, following which Malta joined the EU in 2004. This convoluted road to membership has made the country keenly aware of the intricacies involved with pre-membership adaptations, the need to maintain public engagement, the impact of geopolitics as well as the centrality of maintaining the Union's interest in any applicant's bid. That said, and not surprisingly, Malta is not overly engaged with the EU's enlargement policy.

Southern Rather Than Eastern Enlargement

As the EU's smallest Member State situated in the central Mediterranean, midway between Italy and Libya, Malta tends to be highly selective in terms of the policy issues it focuses upon at an EU level. Enlargement is not one of those priority areas.

M. Harwood (✉)
Institute for European Studies, University of Malta, Msida, Malta
e-mail: mark.harwood@um.edu.mt

Conscious of Malta's limited potential to impact the EU's external relations beyond the Mediterranean, it has consistently adopted a supportive role *vis-à-vis* applicant States. In terms of the seven candidate countries, Malta has expressed its support for each joining the Union, invariably stating that enlargement has helped 'unite us further', making the EU 'richer, more stable, especially post-Brexit'. That said, Malta has viewed each applicant within the context of its own desire for the Union to shift its gaze southwards, referencing how the Western Balkans and Türkiye were important for Euro-Mediterranean security and prosperity. As stated by the Maltese Foreign Minister in 2021, 'we are concerned that not enough attention is being paid to Southern Europe, the Mediterranean and Africa'. Hence, enlargement South is seen as desirable (with Malta providing tangible assistance to applicant States) though Malta's support is largely regional with the government being less vocal when discussing the prospects of Eastern enlargement and Ukraine joining while also precluding any discussion of fast-track membership.

For Malta, Ukraine opens a door in terms of EU enlargement that the country would have preferred to remain shut. While Malta is supportive of candidate countries, any future enlargement beyond the Euro-Mediterranean region represents little added value in Maltese terms, while diluting the voice of small States even further as well as placing stress on a political system with which Malta is relatively happy. While expansion eastward may help to consolidate EU influence (and protect against the incursion of States such as China and Russia), any potential benefits are not seen as being able to deliver greater stability or security to the Euro-Mediterranean region. Furthermore, the war in Ukraine appears to have initiated proposals for increased military cooperation, an area where Malta's neutrality limits participation.

These considerations are reflected in popular perception; Malta tends to show levels of concern regarding external matters which are lower than the EU average. When asked in 2021 about promoting peace and democracy beyond the EU, only 13% of Maltese respondents saw this as an EU asset (EU average 17%) while only 8% saw competition from emerging countries as a threat for the EU (EU average 10%). Regarding the future of Europe debate, few Maltese thought that the 'EU in the world' was an important theme to discuss (7% versus an EU average of 12%), while the high levels of support for the Union seemed to reflect the fact that institutional reform was unnecessary; in the same survey, 43% of Maltese were happy with how the EU worked as opposed to an EU average of 27%. When asked specifically about Ukraine in 2022, the Maltese expressed support far above the EU average for Ukraine gaining EU Membership 'when it is ready' (44% in total agreement versus an EU average of 30%). However, when asked whether the war in Ukraine showed the need for greater EU military cooperation, the Maltese dropped to 33% of those 'in total agreement' as opposed to an EU average of 37%.

Protecting the Position of Member States in the EU Political System

Beyond the enlargement policy's external dimension, its impact on how the Union functions as a political system is of great concern. More than most Member States, Malta is acutely aware of the calls for institutional reforms to facilitate enlargement and the accommodation of new Member States. Ultimately Malta's own membership was delayed as the Union questioned how it could accommodate its greatest-ever enlargement to date in 2004. That said, Malta is keen to maintain the centrality of Member States within the EU political system, opposed as it is to a federal Europe. Moreover, any move to streamline institutions or extend Qualified Majority Voting further will be frowned upon by Malta. Indicative of this stand, Malta joined 12 other Member States in issuing a non-paper in 2022 opposing Treaty reforms (within the context of the future of Europe debate). It seems that Malta, keenly aware of its inability to influence the EU's enlargement policy, also feels that it is not able to suggest solutions as to how new countries can join without institutional reforms. The only position put forward by Malta concerns its red lines and what it will not accept. The same can be said for pre-accession funding for candidate countries where Malta is supportive, but would be less so if that included military assistance or calls for bolstering EU military spending. This is something that Malta would avoid due to its neutrality and opt-out from the Permanent Structured Cooperation. As Malta moves rapidly towards becoming a net contributor to the EU budget, these issues will feature more prominently in future discussions of the country's position on EU enlargement.

Moving forward, the Union needs to resolve a very inconvenient dilemma. Either a limit to enlargement must be established while offering current and future applicants a half-way house (economic integration with no political benefits), as with the European Economic Area (but without the partner countries paying to be members). Or prepare current Member States for a further dilution of their institutional presence in the clear knowledge that 13 countries, including large Member States such as Poland, oppose Treaty change and will therefore require substantial incentives to shift their position. Alternatively, the EU could oversee the creation of mini-Unions on its borders, providing the template and resources for small regional groupings that are then given privileged access to the EU, both politically and economically. Finally, mindful of its seat on the United Nations Security Council in 2023, Malta also needs to discuss the country's neutrality clause, mindful of EU obligations (and the Union's increasing interest in pursuing greater military cooperation) and the need to address the real and present demand for amendment (or removal) of a constitutional provision which includes redundant terminology (as with the explicit reference to the Superpowers) which now seems outdated.

Mark Harwood, Ph.D., is an Associate Professor at the University of Malta and Director of the Institute for European Studies. Having previously worked for the European Commission as well as the Maltese Government, his area of research is the impact of EU membership on Malta.

The Institute was founded in 1991 as a teaching and research institute within the University of Malta. Offering a full range of degree programmes up to PhD level, the Institute has over 1000 alumni. The Institute is also a member of TEPSA.

Direction East: Polish Views on the EU's Enlargement Policy

Natasza Styczyńska

Enlargement as a Non-Contested Issue

Throughout the first decade of Poland's European Union (EU) Membership the country's attitude towards enlargement was positive among all political forces. This situation can be associated with the 'enlargement paradox' and applies to all new Member States with fresh memories of their own enlargement and experiences of accession negotiations. Consequently, there was a perception among Polish political elite that it would be inappropriate for countries that had only just joined the EU to block any new Members' admission. Besides the favouring of further enlargements which may have resulted from a positive assessment of the whole process, it was believed that joining the EU meant gains in the form of increased security and accelerated economic growth. This was also the approach behind the Eastern Partnership programme promoted by Poland in 2008–2009, which was not supposed to be a prerequisite for Membership, but rather bring the countries of Eastern Europe and the Caucasus closer to the EU. Politicians generally also emphasised that further EU enlargement to the East and South-East is necessary to eliminate any relics of the post-Yalta division of Europe. Furthermore, the Polish government was in favour of further enlargements once a candidate had fulfilled the conditions for Membership. Such enlargement would mark a continuation of Poland's interests and its foreign policy. Hence, the Membership perspective of Ukraine has always been particularly important, with this interest being dictated by geostrategic as well as historical and cultural considerations. Whilst enlargement to include the Balkans and Turkey has not been featured as often, the official government position was still positive.

During the liberal Civic Platform coalition government (2007–2015), Poland was favourably disposed towards both the widening and deepening of European integration. Enlargement (including signing an accession treaty with Croatia) was

N. Styczyńska (✉)
Jagiellonian University, Kraków, Poland
e-mail: natasza.styczynska@uj.edu.pl

announced as one of the priorities of the 2012 Polish Presidency. Soon after, in 2013, the Minister of Foreign Affairs, Radosław Sikorski, claimed that further widening of European integration is a realisation of the Jagiellonian idea, associated with promoting democratic values in the East. Building upon the heritage of the Polish-Lithuanian Commonwealth, this Jagiellonian idea explains Poland's foreign policy interests in Eastern Europe, as well as engagement in creating the EU's Eastern Partnership initiative.

Since 2015, when the right-wing coalition led by the Law and Justice (PiS) party came to power, the attitude to the above issue can be described as a terse 'widening—yes, deepening—not necessarily'. The refugee crisis of 2015 and the illiberal turn in Turkish politics meant that support for accession negotiations with Turkey declined. Invariably, though, the Law and Justice government emphasises a need for the EU to open up to Ukraine and the Balkan States.

Polish public opinion mostly accepts further enlargement of the Community; according to the Eurobarometer 2022 survey 75% of Poles are in favour of further EU enlargement, which is well above of EU27 average of 57%. Positive attitudes are particularly directed towards the Western Balkan countries, as was the case in the past, where a majority of the public supported the EU Membership of Bulgaria and Romania, followed by Croatia.

(Not) Everybody Welcome in the EU

Currently, the political situation is more nuanced, mostly because the EU faces not only enlargement fatigue around EU institutions and the old Member States, but also due to post-enlargement fatigue in Central and Eastern Europe. In the face of its limited abilities to absorb new Members, the EU must decide upon its priorities and the sequence of enlargement. What matters in the public perception is cultural proximity.

Future enlargement is opposed mainly by right-wing Eurosceptics and a minor group of 'Euro-rejects', but the scope of contestation varies. Support is given to Christian countries of Western Balkans, Ukraine and Moldova, but one can notice more reservation towards Albania and rejection of the prospect for enlargement towards Turkey. Cultural proximity is crucial, but not the only factor that influences this stance on enlargement—issues of immigration, economy (EU subsidies) and size (potential new Members of the European Parliament) also matter.

Recent Developments

Russia's invasion of Ukraine in February 2022 brought a change to the ruling party's rhetoric. On the one hand, Prime Minister Morawiecki together with PiS leader Jarosław Kaczyński constantly criticise the EU for not having enough involvement and not sufficient support towards Ukraine. On the other hand, there is a visible change in approach towards the European Union and more appreciation of common policies (especially the Common Foreign and Security Policy). The war has generated discussion on the EU's future and the need for reform as well as developing mechanisms that would allow for quicker responses towards threats and instability in the neighbourhood. Although the PiS-led coalition continues to advocate for less political integration, the EU is appreciated for its ability to stand together against the Russian threat.

Poland supported granting candidate status to Ukraine and Moldova in June 2022. The war in Ukraine strengthened citizens' concerns regarding security, highlighting that a stable and secure neighbourhood is a priority. Rapprochement of Ukraine and Moldova to the EU is seen as beneficial, as these countries are seen as a buffer between the EU and Russia. For similar reasons, Poland has always supported Georgia's European aspirations, strengthening bilateral relations and engagement in the region following Russia's 2008 aggression; Georgia is also a priority partner within the Polish Development Aid programme.

Recommendations

EU enlargement policy should be rethought and reorganised, thereby producing better responses to the current situation. The EU needs to be clear about its objectives to gauge whether full Membership is appropriate, even if candidate countries were to meet the criteria. A lack of clarity in the Western Balkans case means that most countries are already experiencing pre-enlargement fatigue, which leaves a window of opportunity open for other actors such as Russia, China, Turkey or the Gulf States. Moreover, the situation is dynamic, as the COVID-19 pandemic has opened up space for a 'battle of narratives' between China and the Western democracies.

Conversely, the EU must not give up its minimum requirements and must emphasise European values; without this, we can build a close economic association, but not European integration. It is a challenging task, especially in view of the contestation of values also by the Members of the community. The example of Hungary or Poland is proof that in the EU there is room for pragmatic and transactional politicians, who value the EU only as long as it provides economic profits and the free movement of people.

After February 2022 there is no more space for a 'third way' as proposed by Serbian President Aleksandar Vučić. The Union should distinguish between a declarative and genuine will for integration. It must become clear that there is no support for illiberal governments treating the EU only as a donor and not as a community of values. Perhaps the principle 'less for less, more for more' should be dusted off—meaning clear support for those countries which, as North Macedonia, not only have a long history of candidacy (since 2005), but which have also brought about milestone changes.

It should not be forgotten that the EU's integration capacity also depends on achieving better communication on enlargement between the EU institutions and European citizens, whose positive attitude towards expanding of the EU is essential for pursuing its enlargement policy.

Natasza Styczyńska , Ph.D., is an Assistant Professor at the Institute of European Studies of the Jagiellonian University. Her academic interests include party politics, nationalism, populism and Euroscepticism in Central and Eastern Europe and the Balkans. She leads the JU team in Horizon Europe REGROUP *Rebuilding Governance and Resilience out of the Pandemic* research project.

The Institute for European Studies is part of the Faculty of International and Political Studies at Jagiellonian University—the oldest and leading university in Poland. The Institute is famous for its interdisciplinary approach that combines the perspectives of anthropology, economy, cultural studies, political sciences, history, law and sociology. It is also an associate member of TEPSA.

Portugal: Nobody Talks About Enlargement

Alice Cunha

Enlargement is the European Union's (EU) most complex policy, in that it interrelates with so many major considerations, namely the institutions, the policies and the redistribution of European funding. From the perspective of existing Member States, they neither welcome the necessity for institutional and policy reform nor generate enthusiasm about new players entering the EU arena with different needs, expectations and priorities as well as ultimately more competition. Hence, EU enlargement can be referred to, as I call it, 'the least loved policy'.

The history of enlargement has also shown that while the European Commission has traditionally been candidate countries' main supporter, each individual Member State has sought firstly not to lose any existing benefits and secondly to gain something in return, as was also the case with Portugal.

Good Political Intentions Versus Unembellished Negotiations

Long before the establishment of the Copenhagen Criteria, one of the first conditions for joining the EU was to be a European state. While the geographic limits of Europe remain under question after a long-standing debate, those limits will ultimately be determined more by politics than geography.

Moreover, although it might be politically inconvenient or perhaps nobody wants to recognise it as such, the EU does have a future without any further enlargement. Despite comprising only 27 Member States, the EU is the most multifaceted and deepened multilateral regional organisation. Throughout its history, it has balanced more or less competently 'widening' with 'deepening', but at a cost. With the accession of Croatia in 2013 the EU was said to be suffering from what was conventionally labelled 'enlargement fatigue'. Such fatigue did not magically

---

A. Cunha (✉)
Portuguese Institute of International Relations, Lisbon, Portugal
e-mail: alice.cunha@fcsh.unl.pt

disappear with Ukraine's accession request in 2022, which at least had the merit of putting enlargement back on the agenda, albeit not as a priority.

The EU is a very complex organisation and hence the process of accession is elaborate. While this complexity is often criticised by candidate countries, once those countries become Member States their criticisms do not translate into attempts at reform because ultimately it benefits them. All enlargement rounds have certainly led to institutional reforms: minor for the first and for the European Free Trade Association enlargement rounds; or extensive for the Central and Eastern enlargement. Yet to be implemented are reductions in the number of Commissioners and Members of the European Parliament. In the latter case, 705 is too many and the number does not bring about any significant improvement in either the EU's democratic functioning or its capacity-building.

Strictly on the EU side, the most feasible way ahead would be to continue delivering financial support, via the Instrument for Pre-accession Assistance (IPA), providing the financial and technical resources for candidates to meet the Copenhagen Criteria. However, such assistance should continue to be linked to the applicants' progress and, more specifically, compliance with the programme for adoption of the acquis. In practice, the present IPA and its previous versions have proved to be important instruments in helping candidates not only to move closer to EU membership, but also to be in a better political, mostly economic and even social position when joining the EU. Nevertheless, EU enlargement is a two-way process and each candidate country must show proactivity in progression at national level, demonstrating not only the willingness to comply, but also taking necessary actions and meeting objectives.

Essentially, the EU is a peace and prosperity driven organisation. The Russian invasion of Ukraine has shown how strongly the EU depends on NATO and the United States for its security. Since the idea of creating a European Defence Community was rejected in 1954, only meagre developments in the EU foreign and security policy have occurred. This makes the EU less politically capable of further integration in this area, when compared with its economic and normative frameworks. Enlargement will not change that and nor will it per se ultimately contribute to making the EU capable of taking on a more significant geopolitical role regionally and even less so internationally. Furthermore, it is difficult to envisage that Member States will be willing to transfer any more of their sovereignty to the EU, particularly in the defence field. Perhaps, the EU is ultimately just not meant to be a geopolitical and defence entity.

EU enlargement often faces the dilemma of balancing good political intentions (granting candidate status, say) with severe economic negotiations (such as endless accession negotiations only to negotiate implementation deadlines and derogations to the acquis).

The EU's current behaviour towards the Balkan region is not new, there having been two similar occasions previously in the Iberian Peninsula as well as the Central and Eastern enlargement rounds: in principle Member States are in favour of enlargement, but each of them has its own conditions. Hence, as has been experienced previously, each candidate state develops a feeling of neglect, begins to argue that the EU is not up to its commitment and eventually this leads to a serious issue being created.

Portugal

Historically, Portugal has been a supporter of the successive enlargement rounds, as much as any other existing Member State at the time. Accordingly, the country agreed with enlargement to Central and Eastern Europe in 2004 despite costs associated with the relocation of some industry and the distribution of European funds. This was perceived as a form of solidarity with those States that were facing a situation similar to Portugal's in the late 1970s–early 1980s, during its transition into a democratic regime seeking economic development. Indeed, the country's favourable vote could be interpreted as settling a 'debt of gratitude' for having benefited from joining the EU.

Having paid this 'debt', the country's attitude is not quite the same. Although Portugal agreed to grant Ukraine and Moldova candidate status, it was one of the last states to confirm its support publicly. However, whilst this is not to suggest that Portugal would be prepared to lose any benefits, it will certainly align with other Member States during the negotiation process. Moreover, given the Portuguese EU track-record, when (if) time comes for another enlargement round, Portugal will also vote in favour.

On 21 November 2022, Prime Minister António Costa expressed his government's opinion very clearly by saying that under the current institutional and budgetary framework, the EU does not have sufficient capacity to meet the proposed enlargement's expectations. He warned that the rebound effect of false promises can produce dramatic consequences, going on to stress that while the EU has very clear criteria for the accession of new Member States, unfortunately it does not have any criteria regarding its own capacity to integrate other members.

European affairs do not impact national election results and enlargement is even less significant. Solidarity among the people of Europe is often highlighted, but for Portugal the Balkans are not a political priority. For Portuguese citizens this region is far away, not only geographically but also historically, culturally and emotionally. There is no close connection between Portugal and the Balkan countries.

The Portuguese have always been strong supporters of EU membership. In general terms, despite comparatively little knowledge about the EU and any discussions that may be taking place in Brussels, 63% (EU average 57%) were surveyed as being in favour of further enlargement in the future and 24% are against it (Standard Eurobarometer 97, Summer 2022). It should be borne in mind, though, that these survey results were produced at a time when enlargement was a 'hot topic' and less media attention could adversely affect such results at other times. However, public opinion is less concerned with the geopolitical relevance of enlargement than with the economic situation, rising prices, inflation and the cost of living.

In Portugal, the daily news is all to do with the EU (and hence, the country) going digital and green. Nobody talks about EU enlargement.

Recommendations

The future of Europe may or may not be related to further enlargement, which has been a contested issue, always problematic and never a priority.

Thus, my first recommendation is for a high-level discussion to be initiated about the limits of enlargement, specifically regarding the maximum number of Member States the EU is willing to integrate. Is it time to end EU enlargement? Will the EU ever be said to have reached full capacity? What are the EU's internal criteria for accepting more members? Any conclusion should be clear to all parties involved and end needless expectations.

My second recommendation is to include EU citizens in this serious discussion, as enlargement also impacts their lives. There was never an EU-wide referendum on any important issue (including the disruptive Maastricht Treaty). This could be the right topic for such a referendum, following which national governments and the EU must comply with the results.

The EU may still be the 'best club' to join in Europe, but it must continue to provide assurances about the preservation of those characteristics that made it the best club. My final recommendation is, thus, that the EU should not jeopardise all it has accomplished and seeks to achieve in future at the cost of damaging its attraction or any geopolitical endeavour.

Alice Cunha , Ph.D., is Assistant Professor with Habilitation in International Relations at the NOVA University of Lisbon—School of Social Sciences and Humanities (NOVA FCSH) and Researcher at the Portuguese Institute of International Relations (IPRI-NOVA), where she works on European Integration, an area in which she has published extensively. Her main research interests are related to European Union Studies, the history of European integration, enlargement studies, Europeanisation, European funds and Portuguese foreign policy.

The Portuguese Institute of International Relations is a research institute founded in 2003 and dedicated to advanced studies in Political Science and International Relations. IPRI-NOVA promotes scientific research, specialised training at doctoral and post-doctoral levels, knowledge transfer and social value creation. It has been recognised as a Public Utility Institution for services rendered to the community. IPRI-NOVA is a member of TEPSA.

Romania's Constant Support for the Enlargement Process: A Proof of Investment in European Values

Mihai Sebe and Eliza Vaş

The European Union (EU), seen as a major political and economic project, has attracted the political interest of Central and Eastern European States, liberated from communism's grip after 1989. Seen as a space promoting peace, democracy and prosperity for its citizens, the EU became a symbol of a long-awaited historical breakthrough. In return, Central and Eastern Europe represented an area of interest for the then European Community, both for political and economic reasons. The objective of Western Europe to promote peace and stability in the region coupled with a need to expand the single market set the right momentum to enable a wave of structural change on the continent.

In this context, Romania has been a constant defender of the enlargement process. Talks for the Association Agreement, which started in 1991, targeted its membership goal. Immediately after joining the EU in 2007, representatives across the political spectrum shared an assertion that the enlargement policy should be supported. In 2019, this was featured during the Romanian Presidency of Council of the EU as a priority in the work programme, with Romania being in favour of opening negotiation talks with Albania and North Macedonia.

Historically, enlargement has also been a popular topic for Romanian citizens, with a strong majority of 61% being in favour (Standard Eurobarometer 97, 2022). One example in this case is the constant support shown for the Republic of Moldova's European path, given the shared language, culture, history and traditions. Moreover, Romania continues to be an advocate for the Western Balkans states and Türkiye, based on the candidates' merits. Another example is related to the granting of candidate country status to Ukraine and the Republic of Moldova along with the recognition of Georgia's European perspective, which has been well received in Romania.

M. Sebe (✉) · E. Vaş
European Institute of Romania, Bucharest, Romania
e-mail: mihai.sebe@ier.gov.ro; eliza.vas@ier.gov.ro

© The Author(s), under exclusive license to Springer Nature Switzerland AG 2023
M. Kaeding et al. (eds.), *Enlargement and the Future of Europe*,
https://doi.org/10.1007/978-3-031-43234-7_22

This support is based on a strong belief expressed at the highest levels amongst Romanian officials that pursuit of the enlargement policy remains essential for advancing the European project, given its transformative effect on countries targeted by the accession process. Romania considers the geostrategic value of enlargement for the EU as investment in a united, prosperous, strong and stable Europe.

However, as 'enlargement fatigue' becomes more visible, it is important to continue the EU's strategic communication efforts in promoting the benefits brought both to the citizens and the candidate countries as well as raising awareness about their own responsibility to ensure that these efforts are sustained. An objective and proactive communication concerning these countries' European path should represent a priority for the EU as a whole and for the member states particularly.

In the process of working with candidate countries, especially those from the Western Balkans, we need to invest in building a common understanding concerning key areas such as respect for European values. The notion of enlargement might be somewhat different than it was 20 years ago; hence, we need to adapt and respond swiftly to the geopolitical realities generated by the conflict in Ukraine as well as the extra-EU influences exerted by state and non-state actors. Furthermore, it is necessary to pay special attention to the strategic orientation of these states, specifically how they perceive their alignment with the EU's foreign policy objectives and common security agenda.

Recommendations

Enlargement has been considered as an important topic by most Romanians during the national phase of the Conference on the Future of Europe. Among questions addressed by the public during debates were: 'How long are we going to delay the enlargement to the Western Balkans?' and 'Where are the geographical limits of the EU?' Considering the practicalities in addressing these questions, one issue that has resulted from the Conference on the Future of Europe is the need to use the existing institutional framework's full potential. From Romania's point of view, a priority should be given to concrete aspects of interest for the European citizens, with a focus on the post-crisis economic relaunch, job creation, a fair green transition, high performance health systems and EU strategic action in its neighbourhood, especially in the context of Russian aggression against Ukraine.

For any policy to be successful we need to have clarity and predictability. In this sense, it is important to acknowledge civil society's role in the enlargement process and to continue providing support for non-governmental organisations in the candidate countries, especially in terms of building sustainable organisational capacity. Romania's experience has proved that the funds allocated for the development of non-governmental organisations in the pre-accession times coupled with those from post-accession has ensured the non-profit sector's viability.

Moreover, supporting the promotion of European values in these candidate countries is vital. The European perspective of these states cannot be fully acknowledged by the citizens if European values do not characterise the societies they live in. An example from Romania's recent history is connected to the 2017 civic movements when the public advocated in favour of respecting European values, most notably democracy and the rule of law.

We also need to be reminded that the enlargement policy is both about political objectives and the European vocation to provide a chance to those who work for it.

Finally, particular attention should also be oriented towards political cooperation formats such as the European Political Community, which is not a substitute for EU membership. The EU must intensify its efforts to counter hybrid threats, disinformation and misinformation, posed both internally and externally by states and non-state entities, while also empowering the candidate countries in doing the same.

Mihai Sebe, Ph.D., is an expert in European affairs and Romanian politics, currently coordinating the Training and Projects Unit at the European Institute of Romania and lecturer at the Faculty of Political Sciences, University of Bucharest. He holds a PhD in Political Science at the University of Bucharest. His area of expertise includes topics such as: the history of the European idea; populism; and future politics. He writes extensively on European politics both at home and abroad. The European Institute of Romania (EIR) is a public institution whose mission is to provide expertise in the field of European Affairs to public administration, the business community, social partners and civil society. EIR is also a member of TEPSA.

Eliza Vaş is an EU affairs expert & NGO professional working on civil society and democracy, circular economy and climate change, digital developments and youth policy. She has been part of the European Institute of Romania's team since 2014 and currently she is the Head of the European Studies Unit,. In the national non-profit sector, she is vice-president of the Young Initiative Association, a Romanian NGO focused on empowering young people and supporting the development of NGOs. At the European level, she is working with YMCA Europe as research and reporting consultant.

The European Institute of Romania (EIR) is a public institution whose mission is to provide expertise in the field of European Affairs to public administration, the business community, social partners and civil society. EIR is also a member of TEPSA.

Slovakia's Approach to EU Enlargement: From Strategic Passivity and Declaratory Supporter into the Reformist Vanguard

Matej Navrátil and Lucia Mokrá

The Story's Beginning ...

Having experienced an unprecedented rise in living standards, economic growth and stability over its past 20 years as part of the European Union (EU), Slovakia is well aware of the benefits that membership can bring and has expressed its unequivocal support for enlargement, although the saliency of this topic has varied over time. Initially, any potential contributions to common European policies of enlargement were guided by 'strategic passivity', namely in adopting a rather reactionary approach to proposals. However, throughout the years this policy has transformed into a more pro-active position, albeit not going beyond expressing declaratory support until Russia's invasion of Ukraine. Slovakia has now repositioned itself to such an extent that the country is now in the vanguard of proposing reforms to the EU's enlargement policy.

.... Grown in the Time

Slovak foreign policy in the pre-accession period was based upon a principle of coordinating its foreign policy agenda with the EU and its institutions in order to 'catch up' with other candidate countries. Thereafter, Slovakia has been pursuing a path of 'strategic passivity', lacking any vision on how to make a substantial contribution to the policy of enlargement. Such an approach is quite visible in strategic documents and annual reports from the Ministry of Foreign and European Affairs (MFEA). These are usually supportive and in line with the EU's approach towards the enlargement process, albeit lacking precise steps on how Slovakia intends to battle against the EU's enlargement fatigue.

M. Navrátil · L. Mokrá (✉)
Faculty of Social and Economic Sciences, Comenius University Bratislava, Bratislava, Slovakia
e-mail: matej.navratil@uniba.sk; lucia.mokra@uniba.sk

An attempt to reverse this passivity came shortly after the 2010 elections, when the then coalition government was built around parties that were credited with integrating Slovakia into the EU and NATO. Under the MFEA's aegis, headed at that time by former Prime Minister Dzurinda, the Centre for Experience and Transfer from Integration and Reforms (CETIR) was created in 2011. This constituted an extension of the Slovak Official Development Assistance and was designed to encompass institutional memory from Slovakia's accession period to the Euro-Atlantic structures, for the purpose of disseminating any knowledge acquired during the implementation of reforms to support and assist now prospective members from the Western Balkans and Eastern Partnership countries. In 2019, CETIR was renamed Sharing Slovak Expertise. Its capacity building activities certainly demonstrate how a small country with limited resources can contribute to extending the Union's external governance practices beyond its existing borders in efforts to assist other prospective Member States in adapting to EU rules, procedures and system of norms.

At the 2018 EU summit in Sofia, Slovakia took a rather ambivalent stance. The then Prime Minister Pellegrini stated that the Union must be fully aware of how active China and Russia are in the region and step up its own influence accordingly. Slovakia's declaratory support towards further EU enlargement was visible, albeit solely through encouraging the Western Balkan countries to continue with complex and difficult reforms, despite the absence of any supporting strategy. This approach is even more striking given that Slovakia has high-ranking experts both within the Commission (Directorate-General Enlargement) and on the ground (EU Special Representative for the Belgrade-Pristina dialogue).

Although there was traditionally a strong sentiment of supporting candidate countries, until the Russian invasion of Ukraine, Slovakia was unable to propose any reforms to the EU's enlargement policy or contribute to its adjustment strategy. Furthermore, the Slovak population's approach to enlargement has been quite ambivalent, with only 48% supporting enlargement and 39% against, according to the April 2022 Eurobarometer data. However, in an attempt to express support for the Ukrainian leadership following Russia's invasion, Prime Minister Heger (2022) announced the need for a new approach to European integration when it comes to enlargement and called for the creation of a 'special track' for Ukraine to join the EU. Although this idea was initially met with scepticism from other Member States, nevertheless Ukraine was granted candidate status in June 2022. Moreover, during the informal summit in Versailles, Slovakia proposed an Action Plan for Ukraine and a roadmap for its integration into the EU. The practical steps now adopted in reconstructing Ukraine follow the Slovak proposals, with the result that this universal support for Ukraine's European future has moved Slovakia from pursuing a policy of strategic passivity and declaratory support for enlargement into the vanguard of reinvigorating the EU's enlargement policy.

Recommendations

Slovakia's accession into the EU after the catch-up with others in 2004's enlargement provided space for sharing experience and strengthening the dialogue between the EU and candidate countries. Hence, Slovakia should now build upon this experience and contribute to candidate countries' capacity building, which is strategic for the enlargement process and sustainability of adopted reforms.

Strategic support is the key not only for regional stability, but also for a healthy social, political and economic environment. Slovak experience in political and democratic transition could contribute to overcoming the legacy of the past to create consistency and effectiveness for EU action in candidate countries. The MFEA should focus on broadening public debates and offer both experience sharing and informed analysis regarding the shift from declarations to actions. On the other hand, for Slovakia itself it would be advisable to build a consensus across the political spectrum on strategic foreign policy issues such as enlargement, so that its position is clear and sustainable in the event of a change of government, say.

Slovakia should devote sufficient time to reinvigorating the EU's approach towards the Western Balkans. This region has been stuck in limbo for so long and the consequent fatigue from the failure to be granted membership status has created a vacuum in societies that is easily being filled by Russian and Chinese political ambitions. It is important therefore that Slovakia should also lead the reformist vanguard in this part of Europe by creating a structural approach for prospective members rather than focussing on reforming the EU's enlargement policy instrumentally, as a response to the crisis.

Matej Navrátil works as an Associate Researcher at the ECFR and as a researcher at the IESIR, Comenius University. His research focus includes European Union, organisation theory, study of institutions/institutional theory, foreign and security policy of the EU. Matej was a visiting scholar at the Norwegian Institute of International Affairs. His work appeared in Hague Journal of Diplomacy and he co-authored book chapters in international scholarly volumes.

Lucia Mokrá, Ph.D., is Professor of International and European law at Comenius University in Bratislava, Faculty of Social and Economic Sciences. She is also a visiting professor at other universities in Europe and chairperson of the TEPSA board. Her research interests include: human rights; external relations; institutional settings and enforcement in international and European law.

The Faculty of Social and Economic Sciences is an integral part of Comenius University in Bratislava. Academics and researchers provide expertise in different fields of social science for national decision-makers, running research and popularisation projects in Slovakia and abroad. The faculty's foreign professors, students from abroad and European research projects give it a truly international feel. In the last decade it has earned a reputation as one of the best social science faculties in Slovakia. The Institute is also a member of TEPSA.

Slovenia: A Strong Defender of Western Balkan Enlargement

Maja Bučar and Boštjan Udovič

When talking about European Union (EU) enlargement in Slovenia, this implies primarily a focus on Western Balkan countries. The Western Balkan region is strategically important for the country, both in political and economic terms. Naturally, security and stability in the area are also crucial for Slovenia and hence enlargement in this direction is strongly advocated. This is driven by a belief that the adoption of EU standards and values is the only road to long-term stability and prosperity for these countries and therefore of key relevance for the stability and security of Slovenia and the EU as a whole.

In Slovenia's foreign policy, the Western Balkan region is featured as being in dire need of positive transformation towards accepting the rule of law, respecting human rights, improving governance and creating stable economic development. All six countries need to be strongly encouraged that embracing the EU acquis along with social and political transformation will lead to their membership and consequently that there *is* a European future for them.

Main Activities of Slovenia in the Region

Slovenia has two main streams of activities in this regard. On the one hand, it tries hard at many fora within EU structures to promote Western Balkans enlargement and thus has used its Presidencies of the Council (2008 and 2021) to this end. Both featured special events devoted to the issues of enlargement, where EU Member States met leaders from the region to discuss a common future. Slovenia organised an EU-Western Balkans Summit in October 2021. While the region's European perspective and commitment to the enlargement process were reaffirmed, the EU did not commit itself to any more detailed timeline for accession. One of success from

M. Bučar (✉) · B. Udovič
Faculty of Social Sciences, University of Ljubljana, Ljubljana, Slovenia
e-mail: Maja.Bucar@fdv.uni-lj.si; Bostjan.Udovic@fdv.uni-lj.si

Slovenian diplomacy has been the opening of candidate status for Bosnia and Herzegovina in late 2022. What should be mentioned at this point is the Initiative Brdo-Brijuni, which was launched by then Prime Minister Borut Pahor in 2010 and is still on-going. This Initiative serves as a platform for Heads of States from the region to meet regularly and address regional problems.

On the other hand, Slovenia is working intensively within the Western Balkan countries, at regional level as well as bilaterally. Regular meetings with Heads of States as well as ministerial meetings are meant not only to contribute to close cooperation, but also promote EU values and the benefits of membership. Slovenia directs more than 60% of its international cooperation programmes to Western Balkans countries, especially in the fields of training within public administration and civil society as well as undertaking human rights promotion and sustainable environmental management.

Parallel with the support for EU membership, regional cooperation is promoted. The reforms that are needed in the Western Balkan countries are rather similar throughout. Of course, one cannot disregard specifics, both political and cultural, but a set of reforms in public administration and better governance is essential not only from the viewpoint of membership, but also primarily from the perspective of internal policies. More efficient government can positively contribute to the implementation of development strategies, can better channel both domestic and foreign aid resources and thus substantially improve the standard of living for citizens in these countries. Yet, as a closer analysis shows, progress is slow and often hindered by various nationalistic disputes. Capacity-building therefore remains one of the top priorities of Slovenia's policy towards the region, which also results in strong encouragement at EU level.

Moving Enlargement from Declarations to Implementation

Here, we need to be aware that EU expectations that any of these reforms will be implemented easily and smoothly are often fundamentally wrong. There are as many actors that wish to fulfil the reforms as there are those opposing the changes. With conditionality applied by the EU, other international players do not attach such requirements for their support benefit. In this respect, the Western Balkan countries are courted by the Russians (Serbia and the Republika Srpska in particular), China (Montenegro and Serbia) and Türkiye (Bosnia and Herzegovina, due to its Muslim population). Their presence is encouraging those elements which oppose the reform processes and can turn countries away from an EU perspective. The danger is that a slow and ill-defined enlargement process gives additional strength to arguments put forward by the right-wing, nationalistic parties in the Western Balkan countries who suggest that following an EU road is not a viable option. North Macedonia's difficult accession process is often cited as a clear example of how uncertain an EU future is for the Western Balkans. The war in Ukraine revealed how 'successful' other international players are in the region, since neither Serbia nor Republika Srpska has sided with the EU and remains either neutral or openly supporting Putin (Dodik as prime minister of Republika Srpska especially).

Slovenian government policies towards enlargement are enjoying high level of public support. This can be explained partly through historical ties Slovene people have with other ex-Yugoslav republics. The largest number of foreign workers in Slovenia come from the Western Balkans. In 2021, 43% of all foreigners migrating to Slovenia came from Bosnia and Herzegovina, followed by people from Kosovo, Serbia and Northern Macedonia. Many are now already Slovenian citizens and have their families in these countries, so personal ties are strong and people look sympathetically to their membership. Experiences from the recent Balkan war is still alive in the memory of Slovenians and even though the costs were relatively small in comparison with other regional countries, an awareness of how little it takes for disputes to escalate into an open conflict is still present. Potential EU membership for Western Balkan countries in the minds of many Slovenian citizens guarantees long-term security and stability in the region.

The Western Balkan countries are also important for Slovenia from an economic point of view. They are important export destinations (second largest trading partner, after the EU, with 14% of Slovenian exports in 2022 going to the region) as well as the region where most of Slovenia's outward foreign direct investments are directed (70% according to official statistical data). Hence, the region's economic well-being as well as improved trade relations is beneficial to Slovenian business.

If enlargement towards the Western Balkans is considered a priority issue, neither Slovenia's foreign policy nor public opinion is concerned as intensively with Eastern European enlargement. However, the situation changed somewhat with Russia's invasion of Ukraine, where the politicians argued for Ukraine to be given a candidate status. Especially vocal was former prime minister Janez Janša during his visit to Kyiv in March 2022.

Recommendations

On the EU side, a clear commitment to further enlargement is missing. The argument of enlargement fatigue is something the countries of the Western Balkan region or Eastern Europe do not like to hear, especially not their pro-European parties. A key issue which the EU needs to improve is the synchronisation of messages going to potential members. EU Member States need to speak with one voice rather than raising expectations too high if they are not all prepared for enlargement to become reality. Resolving various bilateral issues during the membership negotiations seems to be a misuse of the EU rule of unanimous consent. If there is a list of conditions that one potential candidate country needs to meet, then this should be the same for all. Furthermore, better coordination of assistance by the EU on one side and individual

Member States on the other regarding potential new members would significantly improve the effectiveness of resources. The recipient cannot be blamed for misuse of financial support if those providing it cannot ensure efficient coordination and supervision. This should not be too difficult considering the EU's experience with structural funds.

Maja Bucar, Ph.D., is a professor at the Faculty of Social Sciences at the University of Ljubljana. In her research work she focuses on research, development and innovation strategies and policies at the global, European and national level as key determinants of national socio-economic development. She has participated in numerous international, European, regional (Central and Eastern Europe, Western Balkan) and national research and consultancy projects in the area of science and technology policy, national and regional innovation system analyses as well as country assessment of implementation of development strategies.

Boštjan Udovič, Ph.D., is an associate professor in Diplomatic Studies at the University of Ljubljana. His research and teaching revolve around current issues in Diplomatic studies and International political economy. He was a member of different national consultative bodies. As an external expert, he has been assisting the JRC of the European Commission, the Ministry of Foreign Affairs of the Republic of Slovenia, the Ministry of Economic Development and Technology, and several other governmental and non-governmental associations. Along with publishing more than 50 scientific articles, he is the (co-)author of four books in the field of Diplomatic studies.

The Centre for International Relations conducts interdisciplinary research in the fields of: international relations; international economics and international business; politics of international law; diplomacy; human rights; international organisations and European integration. It is also a long-standing and active member of TEPSA, as well as various other international networks.

Spain: From a Reluctant Supporter to a True Defendant of Enlargement?

Raquel García Llorente and Ignacio Molina

The Traditional Position: Neither Against Nor for EU Widening

According to the dominant narrative in Madrid among officials who coordinate the national position in European Union (EU) policy, Spain has consistently been a pro-enlargement country since its own accession and feels a natural sympathy for candidates, having itself suffered from the rigours of this process between 1977 and 1985. However, such an assertion needs to be doubly nuanced. Firstly, because in the two major enlargement tranches that Spain has experienced as a Member State (the entry of Austria, Finland and Sweden in the mid-1990s and that of the Central Eastern European countries in the mid-2000s) it negotiated very hard to preserve its budgetary and institutional position. This can be seen, for instance, with: the so-called Ioannina Compromise in 1994; and a rigid defence of voting power agreed in the Nice Treaty.

The second nuance to Spain's supposedly pro-enlargement attitude is that, while it is true that it has not explicitly positioned itself against any country's accession, neither has it attached much strategic importance to this dimension of European integration. Rather, it has tended to see widening as an obligation, the main concern being that the new Member States should not weaken the pro-deepening ambition that Spain defends. That is why the Spanish traditional position has been to back candidate countries' European paths, but on a one-to-one basis and only as long as they strictly fulfil the accession criteria.

Within the current official external action strategy, approved in 2021, 'enlargement' is mentioned only once and when one goes down to specific cases it is confirmed that Spain's position has been rather low profile.

In the Western Balkans (where Spain had played a certain diplomatic and military role during the 1990s and early 2000s) there was even a notable decrease in presence

R. G. Llorente · I. Molina (✉)
Elcano Royal Institute, Madrid, Spain
e-mail: rgarcia@rielcano.org; imolina@rielcano.org

after 2008 as a result of the economic crisis and above all the non-recognition of Kosovo, which has hindered normal relations with the entire region. The complete paralysis of negotiations with Türkiye, a candidate with which Spain saw a priori as having great potential for strategic understanding, did not help either. Finally, Spain never saw the Eastern neighbourhood countries as carrying any priority and until February 2022 had rather devoted its efforts to making sure that Brussels did not forget the needs of the Mediterranean.

However, this relative disengagement on enlargement and limited bilateral ties with the various candidates has begun to change visibly since Russia's aggression against Ukraine. Spain is perhaps the most vivid example of this policy's revitalisation.

Rethinking and Reinforcing Spain's Position on Enlargement

The enlargement policy's renewed importance is both an opportunity and a duty for Spain to relaunch its position, replacing and not limit itself to vague support, adding a more strategic and proactive perspective. In the Western Balkans Spain must abandon its approach dominated by fears about the statehood of Kosovo and an exclusive focus on technical fulfilment of the accession criteria regarding the other five countries. It needs to move on to assess much more the political implications of a negotiation process that cannot be allowed to last indefinitely. An increased Spanish role is certainly justified not only by Spain being the fourth largest Member State, but also a particularly good perception present among the citizens of candidate countries. This is already the case with other existing EU Members in that region such as Bulgaria and Romania, both of whom have very large, successful expatriate communities in Spain. Hence, some possible steps could be participating in forums such as the Berlin Process and rethinking its current non-presence in Kosovo so that the Spanish diplomacy can contribute actively to any initiatives for solving the dispute with Serbia, thus paving the EU perspective of both countries.

As for Ukraine, Moldova and Georgia, Spain should support their path towards accession, without raising false expectations of premature success that could entail risks both to the EU integration process and Spanish national interests. This could include bringing frozen conflict to the EU and posing problems for European security and credibility, given that without these countries' accession to NATO, the EU is not able to offer sufficient security on its own. Spain advocates realistic accession in parallel with security guarantees, especially for Ukraine.

Clearly these accessions will reinforce the EU's centre of gravity shift eastwards in terms of power (within the Council and Parliament) and policies (Southern Neighbourhood, common agricultural policy, cohesion funds, respectively). Spain will certainly become a net contributor, but this does not necessarily mean a worse economic and political general balance with an enlarged EU. Nevertheless, to prevent eroding Spanish preferences, elements of complicity must be sought with these countries (such as those already generated in the case of Romania, Cyprus and Croatia) and the EU's interests in the Mediterranean must be reinforced.

Moreover, Spain should in any case not only increase its presence (opening embassies in Podgorica, Chisinau, Tbilisi and a Liaison Office in Pristina), but also improve cultural, educational and scientific exchanges. Furthermore, links between civil societies need to be deepened and economic ties must be strengthened. These regions could provide investment opportunities in strategic sectors in which Spanish companies are competitive, such as energy and infrastructure. Spain's transition towards an advanced, prosperous and Europeanised democracy could serve as an example for strengthening cooperation and exchanging best practices within the region.

EU Reform Should Not Be a Precondition But a Parallel Effort

In parallel to widening, the 27 Member States and institutions must work on deepening. However, Spain should not defend treaty reform as a prerequisite (which requires unanimity and could lead to a de facto enlargement blockage), but rather focus on the EU's capability to act in certain areas. The current institutional design, except for certain adjustments such as eliminating the criterion of one commissioner per country, has already been prepared to cater for 35 members. Similarly, the internal market has remained strong despite Brexit and the pandemic and supranational policies are still effective.

The EU's problem is the lack of political will in some national capitals to move forward in certain areas where intergovernmental logic dominates. Overcoming veto rights in migration or Common Foreign and Security Policy is a necessity regardless of new members' accession. The most practical solution would be to accept that those who want more, can do more through effective mechanisms for differentiated integration so that the recalcitrant do not block the progress of those who wish to go further. Of course, there is also a need to strengthen rule of law monitoring, but again the problem lies in the EU's hands and hence it is unfair to make candidates pay for the faults of Hungary or Poland. In that sense, it seems that the accession of vigorously pro-European countries, as some candidates are, may rather help to reinforce fundamental values in Central and Eastern Europe.

As negotiations progress, Spain should also adopt a flexible and adaptive approach that incorporates consideration of other innovative solutions, such as: phased accession; a variant of European Economic Area membership to anticipate participation within the Internal Market; and taking more advantage of the European Political Community to develop political relations of trust with candidates.

Recommendations

To sum up, Spain should opt for a style of enlargement that favours supranational integration in the terms seen from 1985 to 2005 and not that of the polycrisis scenario seen since then. Spain should also think in broader terms. Enlargement policy is not just about being or not being a Member State according to the

Copenhagen criteria and all the technical procedures involved. It is also a strategic issue closely intertwined with the architecture of Europe's security and stability, as demonstrated by the war in Ukraine. After all, enlargement can also be considered as a tool with which to confront the continent's enemies. Thus, if Spain wants to play a leading role in the EU it must take this policy seriously, by actively participating in the definition of a 'more geopolitical Europe' that is coming into being.

Raquel García Llorente is an Analyst at the Elcano Royal Institute. She holds a degree in International Relations from the Complutense University of Madrid and an International MBA from the Polytechnic University of Madrid. She is currently a Ph.D. student working on a thesis about the formation of national preferences, coordination capacities and power of Member States in the EU with the aim of analysing Spain's ecosystem of influence in Brussels. Previously, she has worked in the Department for European Affairs at the Office of the Spanish Prime Minister. She is also advisor for public and European affairs at consultancies such as Llorente y Cuenca (LLYC).

Ignacio Molina Ph.D., is Senior Analyst at the Elcano Royal Institute and Lecturer at the Department of Politics and International Relations at the Universidad Autónoma de Madrid. He holds a Ph.D. in Political Science from the same university, an MA in Social Sciences from the Juan March Institute (Madrid), a Master's in EU Law and two BA in Law and Political Science from the University of Granada. He has been visiting fellow at several universities: Trinity College Dublin, Harvard (as a Fulbright scholar) and Oxford. He has lectured or presented papers in more than 30 graduate centres and policy institutes and has participated in more than 20 national and international research projects. He has served as an external expert or consultant to several institutions including the European Parliament, the European Commission, the Spanish Council of State, the Ministry of Foreign Affairs, the Spanish Institute for Public Administration (INAP) or the Bertelsmann Foundation.

The Elcano Royal Institute is a Spanish think tank for international and strategic studies. It is based in Madrid and was created in 2001 as a private foundation. The goal is to foster the creation and exchange of ideas in a plural and independent environment, with a stable and multidisciplinary team of analysts and a wide-ranging network of associated experts. It is also a member of TEPSA.

Sweden and EU Enlargement: A Strong Supporter Walking a Fine Line

Calle Håkansson

Sweden's Historical Approach to Enlargement

Sweden has traditionally been part of the European Union's (EU) pro-enlargement camp and has strongly supported the outlook of a larger Union since becoming a Member in 1995. During its first EU Presidency in 2001 Sweden had EU enlargement as one of its top priorities ahead of the 2004 Big Bang enlargement process. Similarly, in 2009, the country together with Poland took this initiative to the EU's Eastern Partnership in supporting and more closely integrating the Union's Eastern Neighbourhood States. Hence, Sweden has traditionally been a firm supporter of a larger EU. Nevertheless, in line with the overall mood within the Union and general 'enlargement fatigue', Sweden also took a less ambitious approach in the 2010s and start of the 2020s. However, by contrast in recent years the process has once again gained new momentum.

The War in Ukraine and EU Enlargement

Russia's brutal and illegal war in Ukraine has strongly spurred and fast-forwarded the Union's enlargement. Since the invasion, Ukraine, Moldova, Bosnia and Herzegovina as well as Georgia (if and when certain criteria are met) have been granted EU candidate status. In the first semester of 2023, Sweden once again took on the Council of the EU's Presidency. While not explicitly stated as a top priority in its programme, one aim will be to take the membership process forward, fully behind the EU's support for Ukraine, Moldova, Georgia and Western Balkans countries' ambitions. It is underlined that 'the EU needs to continue to support these countries in their efforts to implement reforms as part of the accession process. Reforms in the

C. Håkansson (✉)
Swedish Institute of International Affairs, Stockholm, Sweden
e-mail: calle.hakansson@ui.se; calle.hakansson@mau.se

area of the judiciary and rule of law are crucial'. Clearly the Western Balkans must not be neglected, despite the present focus being (understandably) on Ukraine. There is a real fear that if Europe does not engage within the region, then other global players such as China and Russia will increase their efforts to exert greater influence.

Political and Public Support in Sweden for a Larger EU

The Swedish political system has, as underlined in the past, strongly supported a larger EU. While this support declined somewhat during the 2010s, we can now see a renewed push within the political process. In Sweden's parliament, support for the accession of new candidate countries is strong. Similarly, the Swedish minister for EU affairs has stated that EU enlargement is one of the Union's best geopolitical tools, a way of creating security and stability in Europe.

However, over the past couple of years there has been an increase in parliamentary debate and motions aimed at suspending Türkiye's EU candidate status due to negative democratic developments in the country. Yet, Sweden's current (May 2023) on-going NATO accession process has for the moment decreased any critical voices, as the Swedish political establishment tries to walk a fine line towards membership.

The right-wing populist party, the Sweden Democrats (second largest party in parliament), has also in the past expressed its resistance towards EU enlargement and argued that the Union today is not capable of taking in more Members. These two aspects are important to follow in the Swedish context going forward.

Public support in Sweden for EU enlargement did though increase in 2022. The summer Eurobarometer survey showed that Sweden had the second largest percentage increase in the Union (+21%) since the previous survey and that 62% of the population favour further EU enlargement. Opposition towards enlargement in turn decreased by 15% to 38%. This contrasts with results from the 2017 Eurobarometer, when 50% of the Swedish population were against further enlargement. Doubtless these new more positive results could arguably be seen as reflecting the on-going war in Ukraine and a strong willingness to support the country.

Walking a Fine Line: Rule of Law and Reforms

We can expect that Sweden will continue to support EU enlargement and moreover push the rule of law discussion very strongly, as a country that has stood up firmly against any democratic backsliding in the Union. Hence, the Swedish political system has emphasised that new EU Member States need to adhere to all the Union's rules before joining. Consequently, Sweden will continue to stress these aspects in enlargement process discussions.

However, a larger Union also creates questions about its workings. Certain EU leaders have outlined ideas about moving to majority voting in issues currently requiring unanimity, for instance in parts of the economic affairs and foreign policy.

Whilst against any further treaty reforms for now, Sweden has been arguing for the use of existing 'passerelle' clauses which would make possible a move to Qualified Majority Voting in certain areas of the Common Foreign and Security Policy. This is particularly significant considering that certain Member States such as Hungary and Poland are prepared to use their veto-powers to gain concessions within the Union.

Hence, these are issues that need to be discussed and addressed in line with the ambitions of an enlarged EU. Following the Conference of the Future of Europe, Sweden declared (with 12 other Member States) that it did not support EU treaty changes. However, how else should the Union adapt to a new and larger political community? These are questions that are still unanswered from the Swedish side and represent a looming 'elephant in the room' for the country. Consequently, Sweden will most likely walk a fine line over the coming years in supporting the enlargements process, while continuing to oppose EU treaty reforms.

Recommendations

Sweden should change its view by supporting treaty reform, albeit strictly in line with preparing the EU for enlargement. Internal reform is needed in due time to make sure that the Union is fit for this new reality, especially regarding decision-making procedures. This also importantly follows the more geopolitical role that the Union has adopted in recent years. Swedish support for treaty reforms would also answer calls from the Conference of the Future of Europe, the European Parliament, as well as an increasing group of Member States.

Enlargement is one of the Union's most powerful geopolitical tools and Sweden should certainly continue to be a steadfast promoter. The country should also support reforms towards faster and more flexible integration during the enlargement process, for instance in economic and energy cooperation to support countries' membership processes.

The European Political Community should from the Swedish side also be strongly supported and developed further. This is also important regarding the geopolitical situation in Europe's neighbourhood.

There is a clear need for a larger political and public debate about the role of enlargement and future of the EU in Sweden. This could increase support for further integration, given that EU enlargement is of utmost importance for the Union's future. These issues should arguably be better outlined during the Swedish Presidency of the Council of the EU in the spring of 2023.

Calle Håkansson is an Associate Fellow of the Europe Programme at the Swedish Institute of International Affairs (UI) and a PhD candidate at the department of Global Political Studies, Malmö University, Sweden. Calle's research focuses on among others European integration and the development of EU's foreign, security and defence policy. He has published texts and analysis for among others European Security, European Council on Foreign Relations, European View, the Swedish Institute for European policy studies as well as by the European Leadership Network.

The Swedish Institute of International Affairs (UI) is an independent institute and a platform for research and information on international relations and foreign policy. UI is a non-profit organisation founded in 1938. The Institute is also a member of TEPSA.

Strict, Fair, Engaged.... And Still Without a Vision? A View from the Netherlands on EU Enlargement and Its Neighbourhood

Giselle Bosse

The Netherlands is fundamentally sceptical or critical towards EU enlargement, a sentiment often linked to the Dutch population's generally negative attitude. In 2016, two thirds of voters rejected the EU-Ukraine Association Agreement in a non-binding referendum, which served as further testament of Eurosceptic attitudes and 'enlargement fatigue' in the country. Following the COVID-19 pandemic and Russia's war against Ukraine, Dutch attitudes have, though, been shifting of late. Levels of support for Ukraine's EU membership and that of the Western Balkans states have been increasing. Moreover, the Dutch government has made various historic U-turns in its policy, by actively supporting the opening of accession negotiations with North Macedonia and Albania as well as agreeing to Ukraine's membership candidacy, alongside expressing greater commitment to the EU's foreign and defence policies. However, it remains to be seen how permanent these changes will be, considering that the government lacks a clear geopolitical vision on relations with countries in the EU's neighbourhood and EU foreign policy more generally?

An Inward-Looking Approach to Enlargement

With the Netherlands' lukewarm position on potential new enlargement rounds over the past decade, it has often been argued that the Dutch approach is rather self-centred. Discussions on enlargement are often focused on what kind of EU the Dutch want, sentiments against further EU integration and a notion that the EU will become uncontrollable should there be any further enlargement. Little attention is given to those countries seeking EU membership. Among EU Member States, the Dutch government has been perceived as mostly pursuing national interests due to its strict

G. Bosse (✉)
University of Maastricht, Maastricht, The Netherlands
e-mail: g.bosse@maastrichtuniversity.nl

and unconstructive position on enlargement, guided by the unofficial motto 'strict but fair': strict because the conditions for accession are not up for compromise; and fair because if conditions are met, EU membership will be supported.

Accordingly, the Netherlands has on various occasions disagreed with the European Commission's favourable conclusions on countries' readiness to advance on the accession trajectory. In the view of some observers, the Netherlands should therefore be seen as a genuine supporter of enlargement policy, committed to applying conditionality consistently. After all, the country has proved constant in supporting accession countries financially through its multi-million Matra programme. However, no matter which perspective is taken, a key problem remains that the Dutch government lacks a clear European narrative, connecting domestic concerns about enlargement to wider European geopolitical interests. In Dutch discourse, the 'EU as a market' narrative continues to prevail, with the finance ministry often dominating European affairs, much to the detriment of diplomats in the foreign ministry.

U-Turn on the Western Balkans

In 2019, most Member States favoured opening negotiations on EU accession with North Macedonia and Albania, but France, Denmark and the Netherlands did not. Subsequently, the Council was unable to take a decision and the Dutch blockage was condemned as an 'historic error'. Preceding this veto was a discussion in the Dutch parliament about accession criteria, which found that North Macedonia met the criteria on the rule of law, while Albania did not. The blocking of accession negotiations twice, in June and October 2019, was considered exemplary of the inflexible approach taken by the Dutch government on enlargement. A few months later though, in March 2020, Dutch prime minister Mark Rutte stated that Albania had made huge steps with regard to corruption and its legal system. Hence, the Netherlands subsequently voted in favour of opening accession negotiations with the two Western Balkan countries. Arguably, the Dutch U-turn had less to do with Albania meeting the accession criteria, but rather the French government's lifting of its veto once the Commission had revised EU accession methodology. With France voting in favour, the Dutch government would have been isolated had it continued to block the opening of accession negotiations.

U-Turn on Ukraine

A week before the Dutch referendum on the EU-Ukraine Association Agreement in 2016, Prime Minister Rutte declared that 'Ukraine should never become a member of the EU'. That view did not immediately change after the Russian invasion of Ukraine. In March 2022, at the European Council summit in Versailles, the Netherlands was once again leading the charge on behalf of the so-called frugal countries, blocking Ukraine's bid to join the EU. Rutte noted that it was 'premature' to discuss Ukraine's application because it could provoke Putin. In May 2022, he confirmed that Ukraine and Moldova were still 'very far away' from becoming candidates. Asked about why EU leaders had said that Ukraine is part of the European family, Rutte responded that this had been more of an 'emotional' rather than a 'legal' statement. Meanwhile, in the lower house of the Dutch parliament, certain parties, including those in the coalition government, called for Ukraine to be granted the status of membership candidate. Rutte's conservative-liberal party (VVD), though, remained reluctant. Yet, the Dutch U-turn on Ukraine occurred literally hours later once the Commission has issued its positive recommendation in mid-June 2022 to designate candidate status to Ukraine and Moldova. Rutte called the recommendation a 'reasonable compromise' and confirmed support for both countries 'for the sake of unity in Europe'. The Dutch government's change of mind can largely be explained by the fact that Germany, France and Italy, all initially hesitant, had now voiced support for Ukraine's membership bid and thus the Dutch could only follow suit.

There Is a War to be Won: Almost

'The bottom line is, family is family, and there is a war to be won'. These were the words of Mark Rutte at his address to the Ukrainian parliament on 12 March 2022. While initially reluctant to support Ukraine's EU membership, the Netherlands nevertheless ranks 8th (of 41) internationally for bilateral military, financial and humanitarian aid transferred to Ukraine since Russia's invasion (total commitments worth EUR 0.9bn). As a percentage of GDP, the amount of Dutch aid is higher than that of Germany, France, Italy or the UK, for example. At the same time, there have also been some questions over the Dutch government's ability and commitment to enforcing EU sanctions, having previously facilitated financial flows of disputed origin and served as a tax haven that significantly benefited many Russian oligarchs. Furthermore, there have been highly controversial Russian financial links to Dutch political representatives, such as the far-right politician Thierry Baudet, who led the 2016 referendum campaign against the EU-Ukraine Association Agreement. By October 2022, the Dutch government had also issued over 90 wavers to EU sanctions against Russia, for instance covering ships sailing under a Russian flag to be allowed access to Dutch ports because they were carrying 'important cargo', wavers on frozen assets and goods due to 'diplomatic relations'. These arrangements also allowed Dutch companies to continue receiving energy from former Gazprom companies.

NATO First, But Also More CFSP/ESDP

Yet, despite its mixed record regarding enforcement of EU sanctions, the new Dutch government, which took office in January 2022, has demonstrated a more constructive and intensified contribution to the Union's foreign and defence policy. Marking a considerable policy change, the coalition agreement commits to: strengthening EU defence capabilities; supplying the rapid deployment force; strengthening the EU military headquarters; and providing support for the establishment of a European Security Council. Core objectives also include a reform of the Member State European Council veto on sanctions, human rights violations and civilian CSDP missions. Although enlargement is not explicitly mentioned in the coalition agreement, Dutch government officials also regard unanimity as problematic for such a major issue. They call for an end to suspension of the Stability and Growth Pact along with stricter fiscal rules more generally as conditions for further enlargement. Yet, while the current Dutch government is clearly more willing to support the EU's Common Foreign and Security Policy by investing in EU defence capabilities, the Netherlands remains a staunch supporter of transatlantic defence cooperation, fully in line with its long-term 'NATO-first' approach.

The Dutch Public: Shifting Views on Enlargement

For many years, Dutch governments have used public opinion as a justification, and perhaps even as an excuse, for their critical stance on enlargement as well as further EU foreign policy integration. To their surprise, recent opinion polls have shown that public attitudes seem to be shifting. In spring 2022, almost half of the population (45%) supported EU membership of the western Balkans and 62% Ukraine's membership, while 79% agreed on the need for greater military cooperation within the EU. By autumn, the share of people in the Netherlands approving EU measures in support of Ukraine (93%) was the third highest in the entire EU. Key to these shifts is not only Russia's war against Ukraine, but also more diverse media representations, such as the popular Dutch television series 'Wie is de Mol? (Who is the mole) which was filmed in Albania during 2021, or coverage of the UEFA champions league in Tirana during 2022.

Recommendations

The Dutch government should place its domestic interests with regard to enlargement into a wider European narrative, to provide a better explanation of why concerns such as those over the rule of law matter to the EU at large. Dutch citizens also need to be provided with a better understanding of why enlargement and the EU's neighbourhood matter to the Netherlands and what that would imply in practice. Current shifts in public opinion present a unique window of opportunity to produce a more nuanced picture in government discourses of the Western Balkans, Ukraine and other eastern European countries. It is equally important for the government to talk about the EU not only in terms of a market, but also as a political and increasingly geopolitical actor. A vision for the Netherlands' role in a geopolitical EU must recognise a changed global context. The country having pledged that it will assume a more ambitious leadership role in Europe now needs to set clearer priorities, such as a focus on reforming the EU's enlargement policy, while avoiding becoming overly entangled in discussions on EU defence policy, for example. Moreover, it needs to take the public along, explaining the benefits of the EU not only in times of crisis, but also as a fundamentally relevant commitment in the long term.

Giselle Bosse, Ph.D., is Associate Professor in EU external relations, Jean Monnet Chair and director of the Centre for European Research in Maastricht (CERiM) at the University of Maastricht. She has published widely on the EU's Eastern Partnership (EaP) and the EU's relations with Belarus and Ukraine and on EU democracy promotion in the post-Soviet space. She has been principal investigator of several research projects funded by the Netherlands Organisation for Scientific Research and currently leads a work-package in the Horizon EMBRACE project.

The Faculty of Arts and Social Sciences at Maastricht University is a hub for scientific expertise on European politics and EU international relations in the Netherlands. The research output of the faculty has received top-scores in successive national research evaluations, and its teaching programmes in European Studies are ranked top of their league in the Netherlands.

Part II
EU Neighbours

What Is Holding Back Albania?

Tanushe Muhametaj

The Citizens

Albania is regarded as the East's gateway to Europe and the West. However, history shows that more than simply being a strategic location on the continent's border, Albania and the rest of the Western Balkans may comprise a potential flash point with a troubled past. Former invaders' influences can easily be recognised in Albanian culture, religion and language, which today make up the nation's identity.

Albania's relations with the European Union (EU) have been marked by aspirations for integration, mixed with challenges and on-going obstacles. The country's ambitions to become an EU Member date back to the early 1990s, with an official application for membership eventually having been submitted in April 2009, albeit these aims have been accompanied by conditions which have proved to be highly problematic.

Firstly, a key challenge being faced is the need for comprehensive reforms, particularly in the areas of the rule of law, judiciary as well as the fight against corruption and organised crime. The EU has consistently emphasised the importance of fulfilling these reform criteria.

Secondly, while the need for an effective system of checks and balances, transparency and accountability has been stressed, strengthening democratic institutions, ensuring free and fair elections and improving governance have been ongoing challenges in Albania.

Lastly, addressing issues such as high unemployment rates, income inequality and limited economic opportunities is essential for the country's progress towards EU membership, issues which are major concerns for many Albanian people.

T. Muhametaj (✉)
Cooperation and Development Institute, Tirana, Albania
e-mail: tanushe.muhametaj@cdinstitute.eu

The Institutions

Political parties in Albania have varying positions on EU integration, although the broad consensus is in favour of joining the EU because most prioritise accession and actively work towards meeting the requirements. However, while Albanian politicians appear to be diligent on the outside, the brain-drain and slow progress is revealing them as otherwise. If a small group of people control the country's economy, we are facing democracy's great opponent, the oligarchy. Who is supposed to change the narrative in this triangle of the poor society, the weak institutions or the rich oligarchs?

It is the institutions, be they public or private, that must educate, protect and develop the human capital. This is a win-win game, with on one side well-administered public institutions benefitting from developing a highly skilled workforce, while on the other the workforce meeting its own needs. Through human resource development efforts, there is investment in the improvement of employees, hence increasing their overall efficiency. Well-governed public institutions empower and encourage citizens to engage, represent, be represented and serve the community. As policy-makers, they improve the general welfare of citizens through different sector policies, such as education, health, employment and social protection.

The European Union

Even though Albania and some of the West Balkan's countries are considered officially EU candidates, their progress has lagged due to opposition from Member States who are concerned about issues such as illegal migration, organised crime and terrorism. Moreover, unresolved territorial disputes with neighbouring countries, such as Kosovo and Serbia, have also hindered Albania's integration process. This no doubt prompts the question, particularly amongst existing Member States: if the region is so complex, should 'new problems' be imported into the EU?

The EU generally encourages and inspires Albania to continue its necessary reforms with commitment, especially in certain key areas, and show visible results in order to make rapid progress on the integration path. Alas, it could also be claimed that in practice it looks as if Albanians' desire to unite with the EU has been nothing more than a daydream for the past 32 years.

Each previous EU enlargement had a motif. Western Balkans countries have been in the EU's waiting room for more than 20 years and have seen these motifs come and go. They could rightly claim to have been the victims of complacency. Now, once again, they risk losing out as the international community's attention has been drawn to Eastern Europe.

Considering the recent developments in Ukraine and Eastern Europe, maybe it is time for the EU to rethink its plans. Now more than ever conditions are ripe, firstly to ensure stability and a secure Europe by integrating the Western Balkans and secondly to regain lost momentum in the enlargement process. The EU needs to re-engage with the Western Balkans by providing concrete support to help these countries meet the accession criteria.

Recommendations

Key problems identified so far are the lack of investment in human capital, the structure of the economy and the quality of local institutions.

The EU through its enlargement mechanism is supporting Albania to be fully engaged in deep-cutting reforms that are transforming its institutions, developing its economy and improving the quality of life for Albanians. But the country's economy must grow quickly to catch up with its EU peers, which is why earlier access to structural funds should be considered.

Domestic institutions should complete the necessary reforms affecting the rule of law, justice, the fight against corruption and organised crime, as well as security and fundamental rights. The citizens should enjoy employment, good health services, education along with social services and must keep their institutions accountable. We can start changing the narrative by looking at citizens and institutions as part of the same system, where both give and take.

Tanushe Muhametaj is Project and Communication Officer at the Cooperation and Development Institute and an assistant lecturer at Tirana University, Department of Philosophy. She holds a master's degree in Social Philosophy from Tirana University, Faculty of Social Sciences.

Cooperation and Development Institute (CDI) is a think tank based in Tirana—Albania. Established in 2000, CDI is a politically independent, not-for-profit and non-governmental organisation. Its mission is to improve the quality of public policy with open and fact-based research, analysis, inclusive debate as well as targeted outreach and advocacy.

Between Hopes and Frustrations: Bosnia's Path to the EU Is No Shorter Despite EU Candidacy Status

Vedran Dzihic

Bosnian's frustrations and despair over politics have been mounting over many years. In a recent opinion poll conducted by the International Republican Institute, 87% of the Bosnian population stated that their country is moving in the wrong direction. To cope with this anger, humour is of the essence. There is one joke told not only in Bosnia, but also in the wider Balkans region to do with European Union (EU) enlargement, which concerns particularly pessimists and optimists. In this context pessimists are the people who believe that Bosnia will join the EU as a full-fledged member during Türkiye's presidency of the EU Council, while optimists to the contrary believe that Türkiye will become an EU member during Bosnia's Council presidency.

Bosnia and Herzegovina is a state that has been in political limbo ever since ambitious reforms to change the Dayton Constitution in 2005, thus making the transition from Dayton to Brussels possible. However, nobody uses the phrase 'From Dayton to Brussels' anymore, given that any momentum for EU integration related reforms has long since disappeared. Some experts argue that this is because Brussels was not particularly interested in EU Enlargement for a while, which of late has rather resembled the famous Hollywood film 'Dead Man Walking' than a transformative process. Some others see the main reason for growing frustrations over EU integration being contained in endless ethnopolitical games and battles amongst local politicians, who put their own interests over EU integration aside and rather engage in nationalist politics of fear than in serious reforms.

V. Dzihic (✉)
Austrian Institute for International Affairs, Wien, Austria
e-mail: vedran.dzihic@univie.ac.at

Disappointing State of EU Affairs in Bosnia and Herzegovina

Whichever view is taken, results from the two decades of EU integration are truly disappointing. Bosnia and Herzegovina has been in the EU's waiting room for too long. Yet, most citizens still believe that the EU is the country's best option for the future—76% would vote for the membership in a hypothetical referendum. However, a closer look into two Bosnian entities—Federation of Bosnia and Herzegovina and Republika Srpska—reveals some major dilemmas. While 87% of the Federation's population, Bosnians and Croats mainly, would vote for the EU, numbers in the Republika Srpska are significantly lower, standing at only 57% of support for the EU in 2022. At the same time and as a result of newly elected President Milorad Dodik's openly pro-Russian stance, sympathies for the Russian Federation and Putin remain quite strong. One figure has deteriorated significantly, namely that referring to the question of how committed the EU is about Enlargement. In 2022 only 44% of Bosnians believed in the EU's seriousness while 37% have lost faith in the Union entirely.

The war in Ukraine has of course changed the geopolitical picture and reshuffled major political paradigms in Europe. The impact is felt intensively throughout the Western Balkans and certainly in Bosnia and Herzegovina. While the West exerts significant effort in countering Russian influence in the region and pushes for solutions for protracted crisis situations such as that between Serbia and Kosovo, EU integration dynamics have changed very little. It is obvious that with the war in Ukraine EU Enlargement has once more become more political. Granting candidate status for Ukraine and Moldova raised the question about the EU's next step in the Western Balkans generally as well as Bosnia and Herzegovina particularly.

Bosnia as a Candidate Country: Is There Light at the End of the European Tunnel?

One bold formal step resulting from the war in Ukraine was taken when EU candidate status was granted to Bosnia and Herzegovina in December 2022. This status carried a message to Moscow that the West and the EU remain committed to the region. The big question now is whether this represents a turning point in Bosnia and Herzegovina's relationship with the EU. Looking strictly at the implementation of reforms so far, the country certainly did not earn the candidate status, but nevertheless this decision was long overdue. Yet, even with candidacy status the '14 reform points' remain on the table having been set by the EU as a requirement which would signal the next integrational step for Bosnia and Herzegovina in 2019.

Following the EU's decision, no euphoria was evident among the public. Bosnians have been waiting too long for anything meaningful to happen in terms of EU integration, thus a sober sentiment towards this process and the new EU symbolism generally prevail. Indeed, the most pragmatic Bosnian Europeans do not wait, but simply emigrate to the EU, thereby robbing their country of its potential.

Numbers are sobering—a population that amounted to 4.4 million before the war is now estimated to be at slightly above 2.5 million citizens.

The decisive question lying in front of us is whether the candidacy status together with new internal political constellation in the country, which changed somewhat after the elections in October 2022, opens up sufficient space for a more offensive EU reform policy. The new coalition of eight parties called 'Osmorka', formed after the elections, started off with a promise not only to act programmatically and pragmatically but also be dedicated to EU integration reforms. While the first few days' rhetoric from the new coalition looked quite promising, despite the ethnopolitical godfathers Dragan Covic and Milorad Dodik from HDZ (Hrvatska demokratska zajednica—Croatian democratic union) and SNSD (Stranka nezavisnih socijaldemokrata—Alliance of independent social democrats), respectively, reality in the first few months of 2023 looks rather different. Any metamorphosis from ethnopolitical agitation against the state towards new pragmatism and EU reforms is not materialising. Milorad Dodik, the embodiment of anti-Europeanism par excellence in recent years, has quickly returned to threats of Republika Srpska secession. Are we back at square one in terms of EU integration in Bosnia born out of empty rhetorical promises from Bosnian politicians paired with stalled reform processes?

The Future of EU Enlargement: Is There Anything New for Bosnia?

Today, in the new European era defined by war in Europe, enlargement has become less of a technical rapprochement process with the EU, but more a highly political alternative, loaded with a fresh normative vision of an EU that stands up to protect the European continent from military aggression and new forms of imperialism as displayed by Russia's invasion of Ukraine. The Western Balkans' fate, where the united West stands against a malign Russian influence, is now closely bound to the fates of Ukraine and Moldova. Yet, big questions remain: What shape would a future EU Enlargement policy finally take? Would it be a variation of the cumbersome process that enlargement has adopted in the last decade or some new, positive approach? What would it entail for today's EU Member States and the EU's internal setup? Would we need to open up the debate on internal EU reforms—including, for instance, majority voting—before any important next steps can be taken? Finally, what is it that the EU can put on the table in terms of concrete procedural steps, such as: staged accession; a new methodology; rewards for reforms; access to the internal market and the four freedoms. How could these issues speed up the process and make it more effective?

Recommendations: New Logic for a European Bosnia Is Needed

The enlargement process' old logic has not delivered upon its promises and thus something new is very much needed. This has certainly not happened for Bosnia and Herzegovina, at least not for Bosnians citizens, so what would be required to put in place a new logic here?

As mentioned at the outset of this chapter, Bosnia and Herzegovina has been stuck in EU integration limbo for years with no real progress. The country needs bold constitutional changes to make it more functional, citizen-centred and thus EU-ready. These changes would require a radical shift from representation and governance based on ethnic representation towards a citizen-based constitution and political competition. Even though it sounds like a utopian request today, the EU working together with progressive forces in Bosnia should try to embrace and realise this concept.

A unanimous Western approach to resolving the political conundrum in Bosnia and Herzegovina is very much needed. Close coordination between the USA and the EU should focus on stopping the negative political cycle, while providing incentives for pro-European political forces to prevail. An important first step would be the introduction of a fully transparent electronic voting system.

The sticks and carrots approach regarding EU integration has not delivered anything in Bosnia and Herzegovina so far. Thicker sticks for those responsible for rising tensions, nationalist rhetoric, corruption and political blockades are needed as much as bigger and more clearly defined carrots for the country once it decisively embarks on the path towards reforms.

Vedran Dzihic, Ph.D., is currently Senior Researcher at oiip—Austrian Institute for International Affairs, Senior Lecturer at the Institute for Political Sciences, University of Vienna as well as the University of Applied Arts, Vienna and Co-Director of the Center for Advanced Studies, South East Europe at the University of Rijeka. He is one of the co-founders and board member of the IDESE—Institute for Democratic Engagement Southeast Europe, Belgrade as well as member of BIEPAG (Balkans in Europe Policy Advisory Group).

The oiip is Austria's leading institute on international politics and positions itself at the juncture between academic and policy-oriented research.

Seizing the EU Enlargement Momentum: Georgia's Prospects for Joining the European Family

Irakli Sirbiladze, Mariam Khotenashvili, and Elene Panchulidze

Georgia's relations with the European Union (EU) have undergone the phases of partnership, cooperation and association, finally arriving at the near-ultimate point in 2022: recognition of its European perspective by the EU. This decision, determined primarily by Russia's invasion of Ukraine, effectively removed any ambiguity regarding the so-called Associated Trio's ambitions, namely Georgia, Moldova and Ukraine.

To ensure Georgia's progress on its EU path, it is crucial that political actors make a greater effort to address unhealthy polarisation and the influence of vested interests. At the same time, a clearer strategic orientation and sense of purpose should be demonstrated by undertaking reforms in key areas identified by the EU.

Georgia's EU Journey

Georgia has benefitted greatly from an ever-increasing political, economic, sectoral and societal engagement with the EU. Politically, over the decades Georgia's electoral democracy has been locked into a cycle of iterative breakthroughs and deteriorations. However, its aspirations for democratic consolidation and membership in Western institutions have been unwavering. Georgia fares relatively well in terms of policy approximation with the EU, while its pro-EU public—over 80% consistently express support for membership—effectively wields a veto on governments' efforts to deviate from European aspirations. The power of pro-European Georgian people was aptly demonstrated by the protests in March

---

I. Sirbiladze (✉) · E. Panchulidze
PMC Research Centre, Tbilisi, Georgia
e-mail: elene.panchulidze@coleurope.eu

M. Khotenashvili
Trans European Policy Studies Association, Brussels, Belgium
e-mail: mariam.khotenashvili@tepsa.eu

2023 against the government's efforts to adopt a Russia-inspired law on Foreign Agents that was widely seen as incompatible with EU legislation and values.

In terms of economic and sectoral integration, Georgia's engagement with the EU has been deepening, particularly since its signing of the Association Agreement and Deep and Comprehensive Free Trade Area (DCFTA) in 2014. Through DCFTA, Georgia has implemented various reforms and approximated its legislation with the EU in many areas. Although the EU overall remains Georgia's top trading partner, the country is economically substantially dependent on neighbouring countries, particularly Türkiye and Russia. That partly explains Georgia's refusal to impose bilateral economic sanctions on Russia following the war in Ukraine. While DCFTA's economic impact has to date been modest, it has helped to improve the economic climate and is poised to bring further trade and economic benefits in the long run. In terms of sectoral integration, Georgia's participation in many EU programmes and agencies is likely to expand as Georgia becomes part of the EU's enlargement policy.

Societally, people to people ties between the two polities have reached new heights. The visa-free regime with the EU's Schengen Area members as well as the educational, cultural and other opportunities have made the EU more personal and accessible for an increasing number of Georgians. To reciprocate, greater efforts could be invested in helping the European public learn more about Georgia, its culture and politics.

From European Perspective to Candidate Status and Beyond

While geopolitical developments have prompted the EU to confirm Georgia's European Perspective, its candidate status will largely depend on satisfactorily fulfilling 12 priorities outlined by the European Commission. The clarity of purpose on delivering fundamental reforms and on aligning with the EU remains foundational for Georgia's future in the EU.

Georgia needs to address two specific overarching issues: unhealthy polarisation and (de)oligarchisation. In terms of the former, Georgia's key political actors have failed to come together in pursuing common goals for EU integration, including collaborating to address the 12 priorities. The country's political landscape remains tense as opposition members fail to respond to the growing undemocratic practices of the ruling party effectively. The problem of oligarchisation stands in the way of Georgia's commitment to reforms in the areas that are fundamental to the EU as a polity, notably the rule of law, human rights and an independent judiciary. Hence, the coming parliamentary elections in 2024 will test Georgia's commitment to democracy and its institutional strength.

Georgia's ambiguous strategic orientation *vis-à-vis* Russia's war against Ukraine has also exposed the country to a certain amount of EU mistrust. While a cautious approach may be explained by Russia's threat, the ruling party is justifying itself by reproducing anti-Western discourses and seeking to apply a Russian-style authoritarian model of restricting the work of civil society organisations and media platforms. Following the war in Ukraine, which has led to more than a hundred thousand of Russian citizens moving to Georgia, Georgia has continued to trade with Russia, further deepening its economic dependence. Through its occupation of Georgian territories, economic leverage and open threats of aggression, Russia is seeking to thwart Georgia's EU and NATO membership aspirations.

EU Enlargement: More Aspirants on the Horizon?

The EU's decision to grant candidate status to Ukraine and Moldova and potential candidate status to Georgia has fuelled new questions in Member State capitals. Although considered one of the Union's successes, the EU's enlargement policy has long been kept off its agenda, with many reasons having been cited: internal challenges; Brexit; as well as the population's fatigue with this issue. Russia's invasion of Ukraine quickly re-opened debates, inter alia: the issue of absorption capacity; Eastern partners' political commitment; and the EU's commitment to long-waiting countries in the Western Balkans.

One issue raised frequently in this new context relates to the eventual extent of enlargement. However, the fear of 'infinite enlargement'—still very much found in some EU capitals—is false. Of the European Neighbourhood Policy countries, only these three current applicants are relevant to any enlargement discussion, there being no other states in the Southern Neighbourhood which will be qualified to apply for EU membership. Countries such as Armenia, Azerbaijan and Belarus have never demonstrated any aspirations to join the Union.

The Association Trio should not be perceived as a challenge to Western Balkans' accession, but rather as two parallel processes in two regions of the EU's neighbourhood, reflecting the high geopolitical interests at stake. A clear prospect of extending EU borders to the East has now been taken up again within the Union's enlargement debate and provides much-needed political significance for Eastern partners in their pursuit of democratic consolidation.

Recommendations

The government of Georgia could do much more to fulfil the 12 priorities outlined by the European Commission, including addressing the perception of politicised justice, pursuing de-oligarchisation and refraining from imposing punitive fines on the media critical of the government.

In order to exert transformative power, the EU should actively engage with Georgian decision-makers and broader civil society. A wait-and-see approach is unlikely to bring many results. If the EU wants to see progress, it will need to be franker and more outspoken on issues where progress is lacking. Simply observing the implementation of conditions and taking stock in a final report will not suffice: a more visible EU presence in public discourse is needed, explaining widely Georgia's

European prospects and risks associated with non-implementation of the 12 priorities.

It is also important that the EU confronts pro-Russian narratives more assertively. The EU should consider increasing support for those who do stand up for European values and support Ukraine's resistance: More funding could go directly to civil society, for media literacy training to fill information space with fact-based narratives.

Georgia has a democratic societal fabric. Preconditions do exist for building a stable democratic state, but Russia's active interference in Georgia's domestic politics needs to be counterbalanced. To help Georgia, stay and advance on the European track, the EU should use a broader range of instruments, including signalling the possibility of applying sanctions on key decision-makers in case they drift closer to Russia by attempting a Russia-style authoritarian model of societal control or fail to ensure holding the 2024 elections in a free and fair manner.

Irakli Sirbiladze is Affiliated Researcher at the PMC Research Centre and holds an MA degree in International Relations from Queen Mary University of London. His research interests include Georgia's foreign policy, sovereignty and self-determination norms as well as Hegemonic Studies.

Mariam Khotenashvili is Executive Director of the Trans European Policy Studies Association (TEPSA) and the host of #EuropeChats. Her research focuses on the EU's policy towards its Eastern Neighbourhood.

Elene Panchulidze is Affiliated Researcher at PMC Research Centre. Her research focuses on democratisation, gender, civil society and European integration. She represents PMC in the Trans European Policy Studies Association (TEPSA).

Founded in 2010, the PMC Research Centre undertakes studies in the fields of economics, politics, energy, good governance and social security. By combining global and local expertise, the Centre elaborates research-based policy options focused on economic development and accountable and transparent democratic governance. Through international cooperation, research and advocacy activities, PMC brings together representatives of academia, CSOs, government and industry. The Centre is also a member of TEPSA.

The Trans European Policy Studies Association (TEPSA) is the first transeuropean research network in the field of European affairs, established in 1974. It consists of leading research institutes in the field of European affairs throughout Europe, with an office in Brussels. Over the years it has steadily increased its membership in response to the European Union's enlargement rounds. Today TEPSA consists of 47 Member Institutes and Associate Members located in 37 European countries.

Iceland's Passive Supportive Approach: Vocal with Others on Ukraine

Baldur Thorhallsson

European Union (EU) enlargement affects Iceland directly due to its membership of the European Economic Area (EEA). Iceland, a founding member of NATO, has expressed its support for countries as they push to advance their Euro-Atlantic aspirations, namely joining NATO and the EU. However, the Icelandic government has not explicitly expressed a specific policy regarding enlargement or candidate countries' accession since it is not an EU Member. Accordingly, Iceland has chosen not to take a vocal stand on the prospect of EEA enlargement, despite the considerable impact that any extension to the Western Balkans or Türkiye would have here, which seems to be in line with Iceland's reactive approach within the EEA. However, the aspiration of Ukraine and Georgia to join the EU/EEA has signalled an exception. Over the years, Iceland has been a firm supporter of nations/countries' rights to choose their own destiny, such as the Baltic states, Israel and Palestine.

Not an Agenda Item in the Alþingi

EU enlargement (including Western Balkans, Eastern Neighbourhood and Türkiye) has been neither on the Alþingis' (the Icelandic national Parliament) nor the government's agenda. However, in a recent debate about a parliamentary bill proposing a referendum in Iceland on the continuation of its EU membership negotiations, a Europhile from the Social Democratic Alliance (SDA) mentioned the prospect of Ukraine and Moldova joining the EU in their attempts to become formal members of the Europe's democratic block. Another Member of Parliament from the centre right Independence Party, a staunch opponent of Iceland's EU membership, slammed the pro-European opposition in Parliament for using the war in Ukraine to advocate their course. This is a common criticism made by

---

B. Thorhallsson (✉)
Institute of International Affairs, University of Iceland, Reykjavík, Iceland
e-mail: baldurt@hi.is

© The Author(s), under exclusive license to Springer Nature Switzerland AG 2023
M. Kaeding et al. (eds.), *Enlargement and the Future of Europe*,
https://doi.org/10.1007/978-3-031-43234-7_31

Icelandic Eurosceptics of Europhiles' attempts to raise the EU membership question in relation to Russia's invasion of Ukraine. Otherwise, the Alþingi is silent on the question of enlargement except for occasional debates on whether Iceland should continue its accession process, as mentioned above. For the first time since 2010 (after the Ice-save issue came up in the middle of Iceland's accession process), following Russia's invasion of Ukraine, opinion polls show Icelanders more in favour than against EU accession. The small opposition Liberal Reform Party has stepped up its campaign to pursue the country's accession process, but the SDA under a new leader has side-lined the issue in favour of more traditional social democratic causes and is flying high in the polls. The governing parties, the Independence Party, the Progressive Party and the Left Green Movement firmly oppose suggestions of continuing with EU accession.

General Diplomatic Support

The Icelandic government finds it of importance that countries seeking EU membership and existing EU Member States know of its general support both regarding NATO and the EU. Nevertheless, the government will most often make such statements in general diplomatic terms within the NATO framework, that is, it will emphasise solidarity with them in relation to Russian aggression and support any efforts to advance their Euro-Atlantic aspirations. However, there are two exceptions from this general policy approach on the question of EU enlargement: the case of Ukraine and Georgia.

Ukraine

Iceland, in cooperation with Nordic and Baltic states, has gone further in its support for Ukraine joining the EU than it has been willing to do in other cases (except for Georgia). The country has jointed Nordic-Baltic statements on Ukraine, reaffirming its joint commitments and unwavering support for Ukraine's European integration and commending Ukraine's determination to ensure progress in implementing any reforms necessary for further steps in its EU accession process. These statements emphasise Ukraine's right to choose its own security arrangements and foreign policy course. Furthermore, they commit the Nordic-Baltic states to strengthen their partnership with Ukraine as it advances its Euro-Atlantic aspirations. One wonders whether Iceland has largely taken such a vocal position on Ukraine's aspirations to join the EU in order not to stand out in the Nordic-Baltic group. That said, Iceland has been a firm and outspoken supporter of Ukraine since the Russian invasion. It has also been a solid advocator of Sweden and Finland's membership of NATO. Nevertheless, the country's EU Delegation is not aware of any position taken by Icelandic authorities on the question of EU enlargement.

Georgia

Iceland seems to support Georgia's accession to the EU and NATO, according to Morgunblaðið, one of the main newspapers in Iceland. Georgian government representatives have referred to the Icelandic Foreign Minister's reassurance that Iceland supports Georgia's membership of the EU and NATO, but this position is contradicted by formal statements made by the Icelandic government. By way of explanation, in the past few years Georgia has been active in maintaining contact with Icelandic authorities to lobby its cause. Hence, this could have led to the alleged support of Iceland for Georgia's aspirations to join the EU and NATO 'behind closed doors' as well as Iceland's firm support for countries that have been threatened by Russia over the years, such as the Baltic States.

Enlargement in the Media

The Icelandic media regularly cover EU enlargement and thus the general public can follow development of the enlargement process in Icelandic, including discussion about the prospects of Türkiye joining the EU, albeit the news tends to be general and rarely includes meaningful analysis. Ukraine's aspirations (and less so those of Georgia and Moldova) to join the EU and responses from the Union and its Member States have certainly been visible in the media since the Russian invasion of Ukraine. However, this coverage has not led to debates in the Alþingi about the EU/EEA enlargement in general, as already discussed.

Recommendations

Findings indicate that discussions in Iceland about foreign affairs are still very much self-centred, largely focusing on the direct and visible interests of Icelanders at any given time. The Alþingi debates only whether Iceland should continue its own accession process and is otherwise silence on EU/EEA enlargement. Consequently, Iceland's authorities generally fail to examine any potential impact of EU enlargement on Iceland's interests within the EEA.

Firstly, parliamentarians need to enhance their knowledge about EEA and EU affairs in order to initiate and take part in meaningful debates about Iceland's position in the EEA and any future development of the EU/EEA.

Secondly, the Icelandic government needs to examine the potential consequences of EU/EEA enlargement on Icelandic interests. Studies on Iceland and EEA enlargement could lead to knowledge-based decision-making on this issue.

Thirdly, the EU should set up proper channels of political dialogue on foreign affairs within the EEA (as determined under the EEA Agreement) in order to strengthen Western solidarity on its enlargement policy. Giving the European Free

Trade Association (EFTA)-EEA members (Iceland, Norway and Liechtenstein) a voice and opportunities to shape statements/policies on EU/EEA enlargement would reinforce the EU's diplomatic arsenal. This would also make the three EFTA-EEA member states more willing to contribute to the EU foreign policy cause and costs associated with further EU/EEA enlargement.

Baldur Thorhallsson, Ph.D., is a Professor of Political Science and founder of the Centre for Small State Studies at the University of Iceland. His research focuses primarily on small state studies, European integration and Iceland's foreign policy.

The Institute of International Affairs (IIA) is a research, teaching and service institute in the field of international relations and European integration at the University of Iceland. IIA is a member of TEPSA.

Kosovo's Leap of Faith for EU Membership

Naim Rashiti

Kosovo submitted its application for European Union (EU) candidate country status in December 2022, almost 15 years after independence. The prospect of joining the EU enjoys full national support, with 93% of citizens prepared to vote accordingly in a referendum, according to the International Republican Institute. It is the fourth application (after Ukraine, Moldova and Georgia) that the EU received in 2022 and with so many now pending, countries so far omitted from EU enlargement are now competing for the praise and consideration that Ukraine received following its unprovoked invasion by Russia.

Kosovo is the only prospective candidate country in the Western Balkans and may remain so for an extended period. Its application letter refers to Article 49 of the Treaty on European Union, which states that 'any European State which respects the values referred to in Article 2 and is committed to promoting them may apply to become a member of the Union'. This can present a long-established obstacle for Kosovo, given that five EU Member States, Greece, Cyprus, Rumania, Slovakia and Spain do not recognise the country as an independent state. Hence, some if not all are likely to oppose its application. Spain had previously challenged Kosovo's agreements (namely, the Stabilisation and Association Agreement—SAA) with the EU and participation in the EU bodies while holding that Kosovo is not a 'third country' (Council of Europe).

Similarly, Kosovo's SAA agreement with the EU signed in 2015 differs from those of other countries. It states that: 'Considering the EU's readiness to take concrete steps to realise Kosovo's European perspective and rapprochement with the EU in line with the perspective of the region by integrating Kosovo towards the political and economic mainstream of Europe [...]'. Looking at the same section of Bosnia and Hercegovina's SAA, it reads as follows: 'Considering the European Union's readiness to integrate Bosnia and Herzegovina to the fullest possible extent

---

N. Rashiti (✉)
Balkan Policy Research Group, Pristina, Kosovo
e-mail: nrashiti@balkansgroup.org

into the political and economic mainstream of Europe and its status as a potential candidate for EU membership on the basis of the Treaty on European Union [...]'. Kosovo will enjoy a right to visa-free travel with the EU only in 2024, 13 years after the rest of the Western Balkans and 9 years after instigating visa talks with the EU.

EU progress reports qualify Kosovo as a vibrant democracy, whose institutions perform those duties required by the Copenhagen criteria. It conducts free, fair and democratic elections and repeatedly exercises smooth transitions of power. The legal framework of Kosovo guarantees protection for human and fundamental rights in line with European standards. Furthermore, the country enjoys a mediatic environment that is pluralistic and outspoken. Unlike many other countries in the region, the Civil Society Organisations in Kosovo function, at least until recently, in a safe environment and push for the implementation of EU reforms. Moreover, freedom of assembly and association in Kosovo has been respected and guaranteed by the constitution.

Kosovo institutions are resilient, respecting checks and balances, but often lack expertise and tradition, hence in need of capacity building. The country has launched its European Reform Agenda, a derivative of the SAA pillars intended to prompt more focused and immediate reforms. Continual efforts are made to align with EU standards in areas such as the rule of law, human rights and economic development.

Benchmarks to earn candidate country status are not solely technical; the difficult criteria are legal and political, as with the Visa liberalisation process. Domestically, building a consensus on reforms is relatively easy, but there is a lack of any clear vision on how to overcome the political criteria and normalise relations with its Serbian neighbour. The fact that five EU Member States do not recognise Kosovo presents a major challenge, which can be resolved only by Kosovo reaching a legally binding agreement with Serbia.

Dialogue with Serbia: An Inescapable Condition

Kosovo has been negotiating with Serbia since 2011 under EU-facilitated dialogue. Numerous agreements have been reached, but implementation is still lacking. Their relations have not improved and tensions often reappear, with crisis in the Serb-majority municipalities of Kosovo during 2022 raising more concerns about the future.

However, in spring 2023 the EU High Representative claimed that agreement *had* been reached between Prime Minister Albin Kurti and President Aleksandar Vučić over an 'EU proposal on the path towards normalisation between Kosovo and Serbia'. Initially inspired by the Basic Treaty (1972) between West and East Germany, it was intended to establish progress towards a legally binding framework between the two factions, by recognising the sovereignty and jurisdiction of each, thereby facilitating the integration of Kosovo Serbs into Kosovo and clearing their respective paths towards the EU. Kosovo had hoped that this would be followed by official recognition from the five blocking European states and unlock its membership to international organisations.

Yet, the EU (and the USA) failed to achieve this objective. Serbia refused to sign the agreement and commit to its implementation. Consequently, Kosovo is less enthusiastic and sees little prospect of any meaningful gain, which may also impact implementation on its side. Failing to make this agreement a legally binding norm, the EU in its Council Conclusions, positioned the agreement as an integral part of its respective European path and called on both parties to arrange implementation expediently and in good faith. However, this is far from enough for 'non-recognisers', who doggedly uphold their position and for whom a full and comprehensive normalisation of relations between Kosovo and Serbia in the form of an international treaty signed by both is mandatory, allowing them to consider Kosovo as a state eligible for EU membership.

For the EU and the USA, dialogue with Serbia is key for achieving Kosovo's goals to join international organisations, earn more recognition and pursue partnerships or NATO membership. Only after the recent agreement (so-called Ohrid Agreement) with Serbia have recognisers supported Kosovo's bid to join the Council of Europe whose body initialled the process for Kosovo membership. Accession into the Council of Europe will help implementation of Ohrid and earlier agreements reached in the EU-facilitated dialogue, including the Association of Serb municipalities, cultural heritage and minority rights.

In practice, the opposite has happened. Over recent years, all EU institutions and Member States have treated Kosovo purely through the lens of this dialogue. The EU is the largest donor in Kosovo, but dialogue between Kosovo and Serbia is the only real agenda; on one occasion, Kosovo Prime Minister Albin Kurti said that 'EU treats me as a Prime Minister of Dialogue [...] I am the Prime Minister of Kosovo [...] the dialogue is only one of the very important topics that we work with the EU. [...] we want to work on other agendas too'. Kosovo wants to work with the EU and Member States on development, energy, investments, reforms and not just a one-dimensional focus on dialogue with Serbia.

Yet, as with the visa dialogue, the EU is unlikely to approve Kosovo's application in the foreseeable future, arguably for poor political reasons, and further conditions it on an agreement for full normalisation with Serbia, which as Ohrid demonstrated no longer depends on Kosovo. As with the Council of Europe, the EU should therefore not delay, but rather grant the status of a candidate country to Kosovo. The EU Council welcomed and then approved the 'EU proposal on the path towards normalisation between Kosovo and Serbia'. This should inspire the EU to endorse Kosovo's long-awaited desire to initial the membership process into the EU. It should in turn inspire Kosovo to fulfil its obligations with Serbia promptly by fully implementing arrangements within the EU proposal (even if the latter fails to uphold its part), thereby strengthening the EU's role and EU membership perspective for the whole region. As Ed Joseph argues, 'no party has more formal obligations under the Brussels-Ohrid agreement than the EU itself', which accordingly has chaired the joint committee to safeguard and supervise implementation of all provisions. Thus, the EU should now add pressure to ensure implementation by both parties and deliver on the agreement's objectives, which for Kosovo will earn the recognition of five 'non-recogniser' states and open its path towards the EU. The

Ohrid agreement provides that 'neither Party will block, nor encourage others to block, the other Party's progress in their respective EU path based on their own merits'.

Regional cooperation and good neighbourly relations are another key benchmark for EU accession. Serbia and Bosnia do not recognise Kosovo and reject its participation as an equal neighbour. Over 40 initiatives aim at promoting EU-like cooperation. Yet, Kosovo is often excluded or only invited with a United Nations Mission in Kosovo designation or asterisk. Its government naturally objects to this differential treatment, but to date has received little support from the EU to ensure its equal representation. The Ohrid Agreement requires Serbia's recognition and respect for independence, sovereignty and the territorial integrity of Kosovo and 'not to represent the other in the international sphere or act on its behalf'. Ensuring implementation of the EU proposal and granting the status of candidate country to Kosovo will also have a significant impact on regional stability and establish a foundation for full cooperation between the six Western Balkans countries on an equal footing, which is key to advancing EU integration for the whole region.

Kosovo has the lowest GDP (EUR 5269) per capita in the Western Balkans, yet larger than that of Moldova (EUR 5230) and Ukraine (EUR 4835). Remittances from the diaspora, which make up a significant percentage of GDP (almost 18% for 2021), have contributed to the sustainability of Kosovo's macro financial system. This large and wealthy diaspora attracts Kosovar citizens to migrate. EU Member States, notably Germany, cherry-pick the qualified youth and skilled workers, emptying the country's labour marker which has a ripple effect in the domestic economy. In the words of a government EU-relations official, 'the EU wants our people but not our institutions and land [...]'. Embassies are not sharing data on work visas for Kosovo citizens. Despite national support for EU membership, only 57% of Kosovars trust the EU's intentions for integrating the Western Balkans. If these trends continue, by 2030 the population of the country will dramatically decline, further eroding national trust in the EU and the membership path.

Realistically, after 2030 the EU can integrate only territoriesy, as a significant number of people from those countries will already be living within the EU. To change this trajectory, all sides need to review their approaches with some urgency.

Recommendations

Firstly, the EU should go beyond mere wording and take concrete actions to advance accession in the Western Balkans. This can be done by integrating the region into the European Free Trade Area as soon as possible. The EU should amend the treaty and allow a more flexible voting system for enlargement procedure and process, including establishing a targeted timetable. EU institutions should frontload this accession process by: allocating structural funding for aspiring countries; encouraging investments in Kosovo; and enhancing development programmes to compensate for Kosovo's loss of qualified workforce and its consequences.

Secondly, aspiring countries also need to make hard choices. Kosovo should commit to implementing political benchmarks and fundamental criteria, not only by full implementing the Ohrid Agreement, but also continuing a dialogue with Serbia. Moreover, reforms must be robustly implemented without further delay.

Thirdly, it is vital for countries in the region to work together. EU Member States often misconceive the Western Balkans; sceptics treat the region as six aspiring countries when these are very small states with small economies and a population of less than 16 million people in total. The entire GDP of the Western Balkans is EUR 134 billion, less than half that of the Czech Republic (EUR 282 billion). Hence, the EU should see the whole region as one when considering its accession into the Union.

To succeed, the Western Balkans countries should resolve all pending disputes, strengthen good neighbourly relations (by meeting all political criteria) and advocate for EU membership together. If common actions are coordinated, the outlook for faster membership may appear more realistic. A delayed EU membership will have limited transformative effects for Kosovo and the rest of the Western Balkans.

Naim Rashiti is Executive Director of the Balkans Policy Research Group. He has 20 years of experience in public policy, research, advocacy and EU & International affairs. Before that, he served as Balkans Analyst for the International Crisis Group for many years. He monitors and reports on the Kosovo Serbia dialogue, regional policy and security development and cooperation, and the EU approximation for the Western Balkans.

Balkans Policy Research Group (BPRG), also known as the Balkans Group, is an independent NGO and a think tank that targets the most pressing issues and needs. With its interventions and initiatives, Balkans Group aims to influence policy change in support of democratic consolidation, social cohesion and prosperity in Southeast Europe.

How Should the EU Support Moldova's Path Towards Accession?

Iulian Groza and Mihai Mogildea

In June 2022 Moldova and Ukraine were granted European Union (EU) candidate status, a historic decision which came 3 months after Moldova submitted its EU membership application. Moldova's response to the EU questionnaire assessing its membership application was submitted only 1 month after it was provided by the European Commission, confirming a strong determination to move forward with the accession process.

The context of granting EU candidate status for Chisinau was shaped by three key factors: the repercussions of Russia's unprovoked war against Ukraine; Moldova's ambitious reform agenda, promoted by the current pro-European government; and an almost 8 years' track-record in implementing the EU-Moldova Association Agreement. This has contributed to enhanced political association, deeper economic integration and advanced sectorial legal approximation with over one third of the EU acquis since 2014. Unanimous endorsement among EU Member States for Moldova's membership provides new opportunities for enhanced EU-Moldova relations, focused on meeting all the accession criteria and bringing tangible benefits for Moldovan citizens.

Transition from Neighbourhood to Enlargement Policy

Moldova together with Ukraine as EU candidate countries, as well as Georgia as a potential candidate, are set on a clear path from being EU neighbours and associated countries towards becoming Member States. Hence, the EU must speed up the reflection process for revising both its neighbourhood and enlargement policies to advance the gradual transition of newcomers into the bloc alongside Western Balkan countries and Türkiye. This process has already started by projecting the first

---

I. Groza (✉) · M. Mogildea
Institute for European Policies and Reforms, Chișinău, Republic of Moldova
e-mail: iulian.groza@ipre.md; mihai.mogildea@ipre.md

assessment of Moldova, Ukraine and Georgia against EU's membership criteria and the Acquis, as part of enlargement package reports for November 2023.

The key features of this transition are related to the fine-tuning and recalibration of EU financial and technical instruments for these countries, as well as their integration in the negotiation and consultation formats available for current and future Member States on a range of policy issues. As such, the EU budgetary instruments, namely the Instrument for Pre-Accession Assistance, designed for candidate and potential candidate countries, must be adapted to the new realities for incorporating Moldova, Ukraine and Georgia. The EU should also reinforce and strengthen its own capacities to deal with the newcomers. Ukraine is already benefiting from a dedicated EU Support Group. It is crucial that similar reinforcements are now developed within the European Commission for Moldova and potentially Georgia.

Opening EU Accession Negotiations: The Next Milestone

The June 2022 European Commission's Opinion on Moldova's EU membership application emphasised a list of nine conditions that should be implemented by Moldova in order to move forward on the accession path. These conditions refer, inter alia, to: the rule of law and fight against corruption; 'de-oligarchisation'; public administration reform; and protection of human rights. Hence, in August 2022 the National Committee for European Integration of Moldova adopted an Action Plan for the implementation of these measures.

Meanwhile, one year later the Moldovan Government progressed in meeting the EU conditionalities, awaiting the European Commission's recommendation for the EU member states to open EU accession negotiations. In December 2022 a reinforced national coordination mechanism for the European integration process was adopted, setting up 33 new working groups under six clusters according to the new EU enlargement negotiations methodology. A multiannual National Programme for European Integration for the years 2023–2027 will be adopted in Spring 2023, which will also reflect new benchmarks to be outlined in the European Commission's analytical report of the acquis alignment in the 33 negotiation chapters. The Moldovan authorities will have to continue putting more effort in advancing justice and anticorruption reforms, as well as speeding up approximation of national legislation to the EU acquis.

The first European Commission's assessment on fulfilment of these conditions is part of its regular enlargement package in 2023. The Commission's interim oral update in July 2023 recognised good progress on all nine steps. Based on this assessment, the European Council in December 2023 is due to decide on opening EU accession talks, but also encourage and provide new instruments for Moldova to advance reform efforts in the accession process.

Building National Cohesion Around European Integration

In the context of simultaneous crises that Moldova has faced in recent years, the EU's unconditional assistance for Moldovan citizens, coupled with many projects developed at local level and targeting different stakeholders (small and medium enterprises, civil society or mass-media), has expanded support for European integration within Moldovan society. The latest polls show that around 55% of respondents would vote for Moldova's accession to the EU, while 30% are opposed. This rate has fluctuated of late and is traditionally strongly linked to support from the voters for pro-European parties in Moldova.

While support for a foreign policy vector is often impacted by the popularity of pro-European parties in power, EU-funded initiatives in Moldova, especially at local level, have consolidated social cohesion around European integration. In the next few years, the EU must not only continue to focus on regional development projects, but also widen its communication and visibility efforts through various channels. Supporting Moldovan institutions administrative capacities, small and medium size business and civil society to be prepared for Moldova's EU accession should also be on top of EU assistance priorities.

Recommendations: Short-Term Goals Preceding EU Accession

Nowadays, Moldova and the EU are closer than ever, working together to address the immediate repercussions of Russia's war against Ukraine, while continuing to advance Moldova's European path. EU accession is a long process. However, the 2014 Association Agreement with the EU and Moldova's participation since the early 2000s in Southeast European formats have already provided solid grounds in terms of EU approximation, association and economic integration with the EU. Moldova should thus explore past experiences, opportunities and linkages. The only aspect that differentiated Moldova from the Western Balkan countries until recently was a lack of any clear perspective for the country to join the EU. This framework, experience built in recent years, is important and will form a strong basis upon which to move into the new stage of Moldova's European integration.

The success of this endeavour will largely depend on Moldova's progress through all the accession stages. Meanwhile, both Chisinau and Brussels should focus on achieving certain intermediary integration milestones: Moldova's integration into the Single Euro Payments Area; exclusion of quotas for Moldova's agricultural export products; as well as approval of meat and dairy exports to the EU market. On 1st January 2024, Moldova will get into the "EU like at home" area. A major breakthrough towards full elimination of roaming tariffs for EU countries. Implementation of the Deep and Comprehensive Free Trade Area with the EU should speed up Moldova's integration into the Single Market.

Last but not least, better communication and interaction with society on the role and impact of European integration will be fundamental for Moldova's internal social cohesion, fight against disinformation campaigns and building a resilient country ready to enter the EU by 2030.

Iulian Groza is Executive Director of the Institute for European Policies and Reforms (IPRE). He is a former Deputy Minister of Foreign Affairs and European Integration the Republic of Moldova in charge for European integration and international law. In 2022 he was assigned as civil society representative in the Supreme Security Council and National Committee for European Integration. Iulian is an expert in international relations, European affairs and good governance, with a particular focus on Eastern Partnership countries, the EU, Transatlantic cooperation and Russia.

Mihai Mogildea is Deputy Director of the Institute for European Policies and Reforms (IPRE). He previously conducted research at several institutions, such as Collegium Civitas (Warsaw), Leibniz Institute for Studies in Eastern and South-Eastern Europe (Regensburg) and Slovak Foreign Policy Association (Bratislava). Mihai's research interests are focused on the study of foreign policy and security developments in the Eastern Partnership region.

The Institute for European Policies and Reforms (IPRE) is an independent Moldovan think tank, established in 2015. IPRE's mission is to accelerate the Republic of Moldova's European integration by promoting the implementation of systemic reforms, increasing participatory democracy and strengthening the role of citizens in decision-making processes at national and local levels. Since 2016, IPRE has been a member of the Eastern Partnership Civil Society Forum and contributes expertise to the EU-Moldova Civil Society Platform.

The Scramble for Enlargement: Montenegro

Danijela Jacimovic and Zorica Kalezic

Anecdotal evidence suggests that the European Union (EU)'s enlargement policy in the Western Balkans has not produced significant results in bringing the region closer to the EU and its core values. The strict and dry insistence on credible criteria and 'fundamentals first' has instead created distance from the EU, with significant European, almost unachievable demands being placed on a poor region, that has experienced all the hardships of state disintegration, civil war, sanctions and isolation. This policy has created a feeling of mistrust in the EU's intentions, which has been exploited by both domestic politicians and contemporary geopolitical competitors such as China, Russia, Türkiye and even the United Arab Emirates.

However, the Russian invasion of Ukraine has contributed to a re-evaluation of the EU's enlargement process, highlighting its importance in contributing to peace and stability on the European continent. It appears that the existing enlargement toolbox is no longer efficient.

Rethinking Enlargement: More Differentiation Required

Given that the war in Ukraine has created considerable momentum to speed up the enlargement process, now is the time for innovation and adjustment. In redesigning the EU's own policy, the policies of global competitive players in the regions should also be considered, as well as the expectations of accession countries and the prospects of real progress in the medium to long term.

D. Jacimovic (✉)
Faculty of Economics of University of Montenegro, Podgorica, Montenegro
e-mail: danijelaj@ac.me

Z. Kalezic
Central Bank of Montenegro, Podgorica, Montenegro
e-mail: Zorica.Kalezic@cbcg.me

© The Author(s), under exclusive license to Springer Nature Switzerland AG 2023
M. Kaeding et al. (eds.), *Enlargement and the Future of Europe*,
https://doi.org/10.1007/978-3-031-43234-7_34

Even though it is a demographically and economically small region compared to the EU, the lag in standards is quite significant among the Western Balkan countries and even greater in Ukraine, Moldova and Georgia. Some countries such as Montenegro could potentially fulfil the conditions for membership relatively easily and quickly, certainly more easily than other candidate countries, if there is strong political will on both sides.

A differentiated policy approach would mean that not all countries could participate in all EU policies to the same extent. For instance, Montenegro could participate in those policies that are relevant to its interests and level of development, at least to begin with. At a time of geopolitical tension, the priorities would seem to be foreign policy/security and the internal market. Instead of waiting for years, or even decades, to implement all the necessary reforms, the candidate country might become involved in EU policies and the system from a very early stage, thereby bringing Montenegro closer to Brussels and the Member States as well as introducing more dynamics into the process.

Faster and Citizen-Oriented Process as a Necessity

Speeding up enlargement is even more necessary for the process's success and the ability to build stronger countries' commitment towards EU integration, while at the same time also strengthening the EU as a dominant political and economic force. However, based on the results of DeFacto Agency public opinion surveys, 54.7% of people in Montenegro believe that the pace is slow rather than fast.

With increasing global competition among important players in the regions, such as China, Russia, Türkiye and the United Arab Emirates, the EU should be aware that its complicated institutional structure and decision-making process does not contribute to regional/global competitiveness. Maybe the EU could take its decision-making policy from organisations such as the International Monetary Fund (IMF) and World Bank, where membership is global.

A citizen-centred enlargement process is crucial to its success. Independent and economically self-sustained voters should be considered the most important engine of positive dynamic changes in the political and economic system. The enlargement process needs crucial changes in the accession countries and as always the citizens as voters form the ultimate corrective force. Hence, citizens of accession countries want to see very clear and practical benefits from EU enlargement, such as: new business and employment opportunities; educational opportunities; as well as better infrastructure (roads, bridges, highways, medical centres and power infrastructure). This is something that other geopolitical actors and competitors in the region already understand very well.

Recommendations

Montenegro is the frontrunner and most advanced candidate country when it comes to progress in accession negotiations with the European Commission. However, it is important to make enlargement a successful EU policy, one that will deliver in the new circumstances. Accordingly, the enlargement policy must become more flexible and faster. In addition, it should become more inclusive, with the active, bolder practical involvement of accession countries to embed core EU values and build strong institutions in candidate countries. Of course, expecting the EU to 'lower the bar', by developing a more flexible enlargement approach, is not an easy policy choice. However, it is of vital importance as a productive long-term investment in democracy and the rule of law, as well as other core EU values. Some specific recommendations include the following:

The Montenegrin authorities should rely on stronger and early/prompt EU involvement/mediation/engagement on issues that are holding up the accession process. Given that the EU strongly advises that absolute priorities in accession activities remain the fulfilment of remaining interim benchmarks in Chapters 23—Judiciary and Fundamental Rights and 24—Justice, Freedom and Security together with application of the Action Plan to address the main Commission's recommendations. Montenegro's government should rely on the EU's democratic and institutional capacity in resolving long-term stagnation and inertia for the overall accession progress.

Montenegrin authorities should respond by employing an accountable negotiation structure with independent, merit-based professionals, whilst creating tangible fulfilment plans starting from straightforward issues and moving to those which are more complex.

In order to incentivise candidate states and drive their enlargement enthusiasm, the EU should consider allowing access (at least temporarily) to critical EU infrastructures for institutions within candidate countries that are meeting and/or are nearly meeting the EU acquis criteria. For example, providing for the temporary and conditional access of Montenegro (as a country with the Euro as its official currency) to various financial mechanisms would significantly assist in resolving issues during an exogenous and symmetric crisis (such as COVID-19 or the current energy crisis). Similarly, the authorities would be subjected to similar fiscal surveillance and coordination mechanisms to those for European Monetary Union's members.

As another example, the national banks of numerous candidate countries, including the Central Bank of Montenegro, are very close to fulfilling the Single Euro Payments Area (SEPA) requirements. By allowing temporary SEPA access or use of the TARGET instant payment settlement infrastructure for cross-border payments among countries in the Western Balkans, the EU would strengthen the Berlin Process in the region, while citizens would have access to a direct measurable benefit (cheaper cross-border payments). The practical advantages of conditional and/or temporary SEPA access would in turn create an accountability pressure from the public (voters) on the government to accelerate EU enlargement.

Synergy and leverage between the EU accession negotiation process and arrangements/cooperation with international financial institutions in candidate countries could contribute to the acceleration of critical reforms. The World Bank Country Partnership Frameworks, IMF programmes and operations from the European Bank for Reconstruction and Development, which are widely used in the region, are excellent tools that could be used to integrate EU requirements as prior actions, structural benchmarks and accelerating structural reforms, thereby reflecting key EU core values. The reform package, prepared with local, EU and United States expertise, supported by the IMF which aimed to remove corrupt judges, as happened in Albania during 2016, is a positive example.

Re-establish country level enlargement offices equipped with the enough capacities to follow candidate countries closely. Montenegro has observed a palpable decrease in the quality of communication with the relevant enlargement bodies since the Montenegro and Serbia offices were merged. In particular, those candidate countries that are pushing forward in the negotiation process should have individual and close contact with the relevant Commission bodies.

The EU/European Commission should re-examine quantifying candidate countries position in the country Progress Reports, highlighting and clearly separating those institutions that are leading the process from those that are contributing to stagnation. Candidate countries' Progress Reports are usually prone to subjective assessments by the press, the Parliament, the government and other key stakeholders. In order to streamline the messaging and spur motivation as well as the accountability of institutions, in each Progress Report one page could be dedicated to a list of those institutions that made the most progress in comparison with others which stagnated.

Danijela Jaćimović , Ph.D., is a Professor at the Faculty of Economics of the University of Montenegro and a member of the TEPSA Board. Her fields of interest include International Economics and European Integration.

The University of Montenegro is a public higher education institution and as such is the oldest in Montenegro. The Faculty of Economics, as one of the most important educational and research institutions in the country, is also a member of TEPSA.

Zorica Kalezic , Ph.D., is a Vice-Governor of the Central Bank of Montenegro with previous experience on the Board of the IMF and the World Bank. Vice-Governor Kalezic has a PhD and master's degree in economics from the Staffordshire University, the United Kingdom.

Since 2010 and until Montenegro's accession, the Central Bank of Montenegro Law is responsible for maintaining a stable financial system, including fostering and maintaining sound banking arrangements with safe and efficient payment systems.

North Macedonia: Stuck on the EU's Doorstep?

Irena Rajchinovska Pandeva

The 'Trade-Off': Accepting Compromise

After 17 years of standing still on the European Union's (EU) doorstep as one of the longest waiting and best prepared candidates for membership, in 2022 North Macedonia had to face yet another obstacle on its EU path by agreeing to the so-called French proposal in resolving its dispute with Bulgaria. By doing so North Macedonia's government agreed on compromise for EU membership talks. This initial trade-off has yet to materialise as it is dependent upon major constitutional reform in North Macedonia to accommodate Bulgarian demands for including the Bulgarian minority within its constitution.

North Macedonia, closely followed by Albania, started official membership talks with the EU in July 2022, initiating a process that will take some years to complete. Aside from the stalled progress of both countries due to various reasons, North Macedonia's accession bid is being effectively held up by its neighbour Bulgaria that as an existing EU member may block its progress due to a dispute based on historical and cultural grounds. Faced with this obstacle, the Macedonian government agreed to embark on constitutional amendment to acknowledge the existence of a small ethnic Bulgarian minority, which can be depicted as integral to the goal of improving neighbourhood politics and closing long-lasting disputes. However, this could lead to additional strain on national identity and even deepen the internal crisis.

Excessive concessions made by Macedonian politicians have already put forward a process of identity transition. It is doubtful, therefore, that additional considerations will be accepted let alone implemented effortlessly, given the continuing rejection and disagreement to move forward on revisions by the political opposition as well as a sizable segment of the population. Opposition politicians have already called for early general elections, stressing stipulations on disputed

---

I. R. Pandeva (✉)
Faculty of Law Iustinianus Primus, Skopje, North Macedonia

legitimacy and conditioning of constitutional change with political change. In short, what seems to be in play is an imminent political crisis.

Two Dimensions: Internal and External

Achieving EU enlargement in the Western Balkans and North Macedonia is essential for demonstrating the EU enlargement policy's success. This could be said to act as a precondition for further EU expansion, particularly further to the East. In fact, as stated earlier, the imposed *cordon sanitaire* on the Balkan states and North Macedonia may yet backfire on the EU by affecting its credibility and influence, despite the high level of support the EU project still enjoys amongst the population, as shown by the latest polls (64% in 2022, IDCSC poll). Additionally, one must underline that North Macedonia is in a much different position now than it was a few years ago when its EU path was blocked soon after having been welcomed as a new NATO member in 2020. This entailed full alignment of its foreign and security policy with the West and by doing so it can no longer be counted as a buffer country to the East. Hence, the external dimension is clearly present, dictating political decisions and reasoning, in addition to the proven, extensive and important effect that externalities have in Macedonian politics.

The internal dimension is equally intricate, given that North Macedonia's political arena remains strongly divided, even on issues that stand as part of the country's national strategic interests within daily political discourse. National consensus is imperative and indispensable on EU integration and regrettably never more so than it seems to be at present. Yet, this consensus goes hand in hand with advancing EU related reforms and constitutional revision processes. The most anticipated reforms must deal with high level corruption, rule of law issues and reforms of the judiciary. The constitutional revision process may become even more problematic if additional political actors make demands that will officially become part of the package. In addition, as the decision to implement constitutional changes needs a two-thirds majority support in Parliament, it is unclear at this moment whether the government will be able to secure this and at what cost.

On the internal front, coupled with pressure to accomplish constitutional revision, this needs to be politically backed by all relevant actors, having been achieved by a comprehensive and open procedure, that includes all considerations. However, this will inevitably cause further strain on national identity and lead to an additional identity transition. If success of the revision process is linked to holding early general elections, then it may be contaminated by daily political confrontations, a danger that should certainly be considered and avoided. On the external front, the EU needs to find a solution for its dissent on enlargement and show itself as a credible partner ready to fulfil its promise. Accordingly, these external pressures may prove decidedly influential, if we are to judge from past experiences. Indeed, one would be justified in being sceptical about implementation of this 'last' step forward without consideration of the external dimension.

The Great Unknown

Currently, in 2023 the challenges for North Macedonia's EU accession remain great and may become even greater as the EU path becomes extended and repeatedly blocked by even tougher and harder obstacles, which will be difficult to remove. Moreover, from experience they will probably (re)appear as the country (hopefully) moves forward.

With no certain perspective in sight, one that will include a clear path and guarantee no additional obstacles, one can regrettably reason that implementation of this last compromise may yet prove futile. Hence, it may be only a question of time before a political crisis ensues, with enough potential not only to destabilise the country, but also produce regional unrest. If anything, those political actors in support of EU accession may become weaker and the context may turn out to be critically complicated.

The recent past has taught us a lesson in delayed advancement which, combined with the local setting, global crises and regional features can very well lead to an epic failing in the rule of law, complete backsliding on some issues and little or no progress in other areas.

The loss of an EU perspective may cause a ripple effect nationally and regionally, since a profound part of people's expectations is based on their belief that following the EU path guarantees a brighter future. This can effectively cause prolonged destabilisation and its consequences can most probably not be moderated without problems since it may develop into a full-scale crisis incorporating political, economic and security concerns. Hence, keeping the EU high on the agenda is necessary as it is related to motivation for reform and consolidation; it maintains that membership may be an impulse powerful enough to halt the on-going emigration tendencies from the Western Balkans into the EU; it is a promise for improving living conditions in which both economic progress and legal security prevail; and it is also a testament that no leniency should be shown when it comes to the rule of law. How the situation will play out in the next months is just too uncertain to project at this point, yet what is certain is that much of the work will need to be done on the internal front and it cannot be done without the EU's perspective and support in place.

Irena Rajchinovska Pandeva , Ph.D., has a background in political science and international relations. She works as professor at the Iustinianus Primus Law Faculty at the Ss. Cyril and Methodius University in Skopje, where she teaches several courses at undergraduate, master and doctoral levels. She is also vice dean for science and international cooperation of the faculty. She is alumni of US Exchange Program, CEEPUS, ERASMUS and OEAD programmes, local coordinator of the CEEPUS network 'Ethics and politics in European context', director of the Summer school on Refugee Rights and Migration at UKIM and member of the Editorial Board of Southeastern Europe (SEEU) Brill Journal.

The Iustinianus Primus Law Faculty, Skopje, is one of the oldest higher education institutions in the country, offering study programmes in law, political science, journalism and public relations. It is part of the oldest and largest public University in North Macedonia—Ss. Cyril and Methodius University in Skopje. It is also a member of TEPSA.

Norway: A Non-member But Active Supporter of EU Enlargement

Pernille Rieker

Enlargement of the European Union (EU), particularly eastward, is generally perceived as one of its most successful external policies, a view which is certainly shared in Norway. This stems largely from a belief that the big bang enlargement in 2004, followed by the membership of Romania and Bulgaria in 2007 and Croatia in 2013, has proved to be an effective tool for increasing political stability and triggering growth in Europe. While serious challenges with democratic backsliding in Hungary and judiciary independence in Poland clearly cannot be ignored, most of these states have experienced both a consolidation of their democracies and economic growth since joining the EU. Enlargement has also led to a stronger role for the Union in global affairs. While some feared that enlargement would lead to more heterogeneity and a weakening of the bloc, the contrary has been the case. The EU is clearly a more important global actor today than it was in 2004.

At the same time, enlargement as such has experienced a certain stalemate since 2013. This has partly been caused by a lack of democratic progress in the remaining candidate states or even backsliding but is also due to the EU having been preoccupied with a series of serious internal and external crisis that had to be given priority over enlargement. However, with Russia's invasion of Ukraine on 24 February 2022 the situation immediately changed. Suddenly enlargement returned to the top of the Union's agenda, once again as a key tool for creating stability and security on the European continent. The unanimous decision by Member States to grant candidate status to Ukraine, Moldova and Bosnia and Herzegovina as well as a 'European Perspective' to Georgia is historic in many ways.

P. Rieker (✉)
Norwegian Institute of International Affairs, Oslo, Norway
e-mail: pernille.rieker@nupi.no

© The Author(s), under exclusive license to Springer Nature Switzerland AG 2023
M. Kaeding et al. (eds.), *Enlargement and the Future of Europe*,
https://doi.org/10.1007/978-3-031-43234-7_36

Norway is not a member of the EU, but it is highly integrated through the European Economic Area (EEA) agreement, which makes the country a cohesive part of the internal market and a series of other agreements. Norway has always supported EU enlargement and it has even actively been assisting candidates and potential candidates on their path towards membership, given that it is in Norway's best interests to have a stable and prosperous Europe.

Enlargement of the EU Means Enlargement of the EEA

EU enlargement affects Norway in various ways. Firstly, most importantly any enlargement of the EU also means expansion of the EEA. Thus, this has direct consequences for Norway, which has been an integrated part of the EEA since 1992, in that it means a larger common market for goods and services, but also a larger labour market. While the former is seen as undeniably positive, as with many Member States, there are mixed feelings about the latter due to fears of 'social dumping' and increased unemployment among Norway's workforce. Some have argued for bringing candidate states into the EEA prior to their accession to the EU. However, this is an unrealistic scenario, given that once a candidate state complies with the internal market, it is also in compliance with membership. Hence, it is highly unlikely that a candidate country will settle for less than full membership in such a situation. The EEA agreement was never an alternative for the UK either, as it was considered by the Brexiteers as even worse than membership: having to comply with all the rules, without any influence.

Secondly, EU enlargement also expands the number of countries that are eligible for EEA grants, a mechanism through which Norway and the other non-EU EEA countries (Iceland and Liechtenstein) contribute to lessening economic and social disparities, thereby strengthening bilateral relations with the beneficiary countries in Eastern and Southern Europe as well as the Baltic states. Most new members are therefore likely to be included in this group of beneficiary states.

Thirdly and finally, EEA enlargement also means expansion of the regional European security community that to date has had an important stabilising effect in Europe, from which Norway is benefiting.

Accordingly, the various Norwegian governments of different political colours and profiles, as well as the Norwegian people as such have always been supportive of the enlargement process. While it may seem like a paradox that there is Norwegian support for enlargement, but no majority in favour of Norway becoming an EU member, this must be explained by the fact that Norway has a sound economy and well-functioning state, which in turn would normally indicate little demand for change.

However, an opinion poll from September 2022 showed a shift in Norwegian opinion since the Russian invasion of Ukraine: Endre Tvinnereim (2022) showed that while there was still a majority against membership, this majority had become much smaller: down from 60% to 47%. Still, a later poll from March 2023 indicated that this was only a temporary change as 52% replied that they would have voted no to EU membership in a potential new referendum, 27% would have voted for and 21% were undecided. Yet, some political parties are now arguing for a new membership debate, as the EU has changed fundamentally since 1994—partly due to enlargement. However, as the current coalition government consists of one political party that is against EU membership whilst the other is divided on this issue, Norwegian membership is not on the agenda for the moment.

How does Norway relate to the enlargement process as a non-member with no formal engagement in this process? Given the country's long tradition of working closely with candidates or potential candidates, Norway has been active in supporting not only the Western Balkans states, but also those in the Eastern Neighbourhood as they attempt to build well-functioning democracies and independent judiciaries, basic requirements for future EU membership. Even though Norway has independent policies towards both regions, its approach results from close cooperation with the EU.

How Is the New Momentum in the Union's Enlargement Policy Perceived in Norway?

Russia's invasion of Ukraine has not only affected Norwegian foreign and security policy in various ways, but also impacted its energy policy. Due to sanctions, Norway has now replaced Russia as the main provider of natural gas to Europe. While this has led to a massive increase in Norwegian income, it has also increased the country's vulnerability as any interruption in Norwegian gas production would clearly be an effective way of harming the whole continent. Thus, in terms of its security and defence policy, the country is on high alert. Norway's NATO membership is perceived by a large majority of the Norwegians as crucial for preserving security, but the EU's role as an important security actor is also increasingly recognised. Norway is also cooperating closely with the EU: It is signing up to most of the EU's sanctions against Russia and supports closer NATO-EU cooperation. The decision to set up a joint EU-NATO taskforce on resilience and critical infrastructure is a case in point, as one of the key tasks will be to protect Norwegian gas production and pipelines to the continent.

While Norway has been supporting Ukraine financially, politically and militarily since the invasion, many have argued that the country should do more as it has been profiting economically from the increase in gas prices. The government finally decided to boost its support substantially and managed to win parliamentary agreement for a five-year support plan. Moreover, Norway is also explicitly supporting the EU's decision to grant candidate status to Ukraine and Moldova. At the time of writing (April 2023) Norway is among the top ten contributors to Ukraine.

Recommendations

Enlargement is still seen as a key stability mechanism in the current geopolitical context—by both the EU and in Norway. However, there is also a broad understanding that this policy also needs to be adjusted to a new geopolitical context. While support for adaptation to the EU acquis remains crucial for making candidate states ready for EU membership (as well as the EEA), more emphasis should be put on assisting these states in becoming more resilient against different forms of interference from non-democratic external actors such as Russia and China. Thus, the EU and Norway should continue to cooperate closely on this which is clearly in the interests of both parties.

Pernille Rieker, Ph.D., is a Research Professor at the Norwegian Institute of International Affairs (NUPI) and a part-time full professor at the Inland University of Applied Sciences. Her research is in the field of European integration and European security with a special focus on France and the Nordic countries.

NUPI is a leading institution for research and communication about international affairs, currently ranked 47th among non-US think tanks, making it Norway's top and one of Europe's leading research institutes. It is a major centre for research on international issues in areas of specific relevance to Norwegian foreign policy. As such, the Institute communicates research-based insights to the Norwegian public as well as wider international audiences, being committed to excellence, relevance and credibility. NUPI is also a member of TEPSA.

Serbia on a Rocky Road to the EU

Milena Mihajlovic

While Russia's unprovoked aggression in Ukraine has prompted the European Union (EU) to uplift the subject of enlargement on its political agenda, over a year has passed with mixed results regarding candidates' substantive progress towards membership. Despite incremental steps in the shape of granting candidate status to three more countries (Ukraine, Moldova as well as Bosnia and Herzegovina) along with opening accession negotiations with Albania and North Macedonia (the latter only conditionally), the EU is still unwilling to speak about target dates or definitive preparation for accommodating new Members. This apparent lack of true political resolve to enlarge the Union has over recent years led to disillusionment both for the populations and governments in various prospective enlargement countries. This chapter focuses on Serbia as a potentially strong case for demonstrating the loss of transformative power in the EU's enlargement policy following both internal and external negative influences. It argues that the EU's path to restoring influence and credibility in Serbia will not lead from direct approaches, but rather reflect progress in other Western Balkan countries where the EU will need to prove it is serious about enlargement.

Two Decades of an Ambiguous Enlargement Policy

The year 2023 marked two decades since the EU-Western Balkans summit in Thessaloniki, which for the first time presented a European perspective for this region. Yet, in all the intervening years only one country made it into the EU, namely Croatia. Everywhere else in the region has been plagued by territorial and identity disputes, which the EU has not been able to help resolve successfully. It has also suffered from bad governance, rising corruption and increasing influence from

M. Mihajlovic (✉)
European Policy Centre, Belgrade, Serbia
e-mail: milena.mihajlovic@cep.org.rs

© The Author(s), under exclusive license to Springer Nature Switzerland AG 2023
M. Kaeding et al. (eds.), *Enlargement and the Future of Europe*,
https://doi.org/10.1007/978-3-031-43234-7_37

Russia, China, Türkiye and other non-democratic actors, all seeking to advance their own political and economic agendas, often at the expense of the EU's. Even the bravest examples of political sacrifices made to advance EU accession, such as that made by North Macedonia which changed its name to accommodate Greek demands, were not rewarded by promotion in the accession process. The EU's inability to show resolve and advance the integration of the best-performing candidates has not only caused political crisis in North Macedonia, but has also sent an echo across the region that meeting difficult demands made in the EU accession process might leave you exposed in the next election, with no rewards or benefits for the people. Even the belated French 'fix' of the problem (at that point probably the only possible solution for the Bulgarian unilateral demands towards North Macedonia) came as too little too late to change this fundamental key takeaway.

The EU and Serbia Parting Ways?

This lack of a decisive and ambitious enlargement policy has had a particularly negative effect on Serbia, a country which has had a difficult relationship with the EU since the beginning of its democratic transition in 2000. After delivering on the politically challenging requests related to cooperation with the Hague Tribunal for war crimes in ex-Yugoslavia, which included extradition of several high-level political and military leaders, the country managed to advance on its EU path and even open accession negotiations. Yet, the drastic lowering of enlargement on the EU political agenda during the mandate of Juncker's Commission led to an open-ended process, sending a clear signal to the region that the Union was not prepared for new Members. At this time, Serbia progressively opened itself to Russia's and China's political and socio-economic influences, while the quality of its democracy entered a period of progressive decline only a few years after the initial democratic breakthrough. The resulting relationship between the EU and Serbia can nowadays be described as unambitious and insincere. Such a description applies to both the motivation of domestic elites to fulfil membership conditions and the EU's interest to see Serbia as a Member State. Consequently, according to the Regional Cooperation Council in 2022, 41% of Serbs believe that membership will never happen, while a traditional survey from the Serbian Ministry of European Integration currently puts support for membership at 43%, close to its historical minimum of 41%.

The Road to Belgrade Leads Through Skopje and Tirana

Considering the dismal state of Serbia's democracy and its current unwillingness to align with the EU's restrictive measures against Russia, it is difficult to imagine that Serbia will make swift progress towards EU membership in the next few years. Yet, to counter malign external influences in its own inner courtyard and prove itself as a strong geopolitical actor in the region, the EU needs a success story in its Balkan enlargement. By showing an improved capacity to reward progress in reforms with decisive advancement towards membership, the Union can, even after two decades, demonstrate its resolve to integrate the region and restore the transformative power of its once most successful foreign policy. At present, the best candidates in the region to show such resolve might be North Macedonia and Albania. They have only just begun accession negotiations with the initial legislative screening phase and would greatly benefit from a reliable and accelerated process that would allow them to catch up with the nominal frontrunners, Serbia and Montenegro, who have failed to make substantive progress in their membership preparedness for several years. This would reflect very positively across the whole region, demonstrating as baseless any growing belief that Balkan states might never make it into the EU. It would also help demonstrate that pursuit of reforms can indeed yield results in terms of drawing closer to membership.

Recommendations: Accession by Stages to Motivate All Candidates

A Model of Staged Accession to the EU has been proposed by the European Policy Centre (Belgrade) and Centre for European Policy Studies (Brussels), with the objective of breaking the enlargement impasse. It sets out to achieve this aim by, on the one hand, creating greater incentives for candidates to press with the demanding reforms, while on the other hand accommodating concerns of the most enlargement-sceptic Member States. Two pre-accession stages would progressively offer bundles of benefits by way of more funding and participation in the work of EU institutions in return for increasing membership preparedness. A third stage would come about with the ratification of an accession treaty, albeit this defined time-barred limitations of certain membership rights, most notably the right to veto EU decisions in unanimity-governed matters. The same stage would entail similarly time-barred post-accession monitoring and conditioning focused on fundamental EU values (Article 2 of the Treaty on European Union), for which the EU currently lacks functional protection mechanisms, due to the cumbersome Article 7 conditionality. Once temporary derogations expire, new Member States become conventional members (fourth stage), with rights and obligations matching those of all others.

Thus, these limited derogations would represent a token of good will by candidates to ensure membership happens for them even if the EU does not manage to prepare itself fully for enlargement in the coming few years. At the same time, they would provide the Union with a grace period of another 10–15 years, say, to finalise the demanding internal reforms. While it is true that at the end of that period an unreformed EU would possibly become slightly more dysfunctional than it is with 27 Members, the pressure of expiring derogations could well provide the right push for Member States to agree on the way forward towards a better EU.

Meanwhile, such a politically unclogged enlargement policy, strongly driven by the European Commission and followed by Member States with a sense of responsibility for the EU's strategic autonomy, would expose Western Balkan leaders' commitment to pursue membership with substantial reforms. It would leave little remaining space for playing the political blame-game with Brussels. Consequently, Serbia's political leadership would have to commit to extending full support to the EU's foreign policy and press on with the necessary reforms in order to seize the day and remain a frontrunner in a speedier and more competitive race towards EU membership.

Milena Lazarevic is one of the founders and Programme Director of European Policy Centre (CEP), an independent, non-governmental, think tank based in Belgrade, Serbia. She is co-author of the Template for a Staged Accession to the European Union, a comprehensive proposal for reforming the EU's enlargement policy to accommodate prompter accession for the Western Balkan countries.

European Policy Centre (Centar za evropske politike—CEP) is a non-governmental, non-profit, independent think tank, founded by a group of professionals in the area of EU law, EU affairs, economics and public administration reform, with a shared vision of changing the policy making environment in Serbia for the better—by rendering it more evidence based, more open and inclusive and more substantially EU accession driven.

Switzerland: Not a Candidate But a Partner in EU Enlargement

Frank Schimmelfennig

As concerns European Union (EU) enlargement, Switzerland appears to be the ultimate fence-sitter, with the country lacking any ambition to become a Member. In 2016, the Swiss government formally withdrew its request for admission that it had filed in 1992, but which had been turned into a 'dead letter' after the negative European Economic Area referendum during December of that year. For a long time, public opinion polls have shown consistently that only a small minority of Swiss respondents, typically around 15%, are in favour of EU accession. Consequently, Switzerland has no formal stake or role in either the EU's enlargement decision-making or its process. Yet, Switzerland *is* affected and involved. Moreover, it is an important partner for the EU in supporting the European integration of Eastern Europe.

Markets and Migration: How Switzerland Is Affected by Enlargement

As with European integration in general, EU enlargement positively impacts Switzerland, a country in the geographic centre of Europe, which is not only highly interconnected and interdependent with the EU, but also has broad access to the EU's internal market and public policies. For example, enlargement promotes peace, political stability, quality of government and economic liberalisation. Moreover, it expands markets and cooperation. As an outward-oriented economy, Switzerland certainly stands to benefit from the promotion of market integration, regulatory quality and administrative capacity in the accession countries.

Even though in geographical terms Switzerland is relatively remote from the accession countries, it is significantly affected, not least through migration.

F. Schimmelfennig (✉)
ETH Zurich, Zurich, Switzerland
e-mail: frank.schimmelfennig@eup.gess.ethz.ch

Switzerland has, for example, been a major destination country for post-Yugoslav emigration, with 180,000 residents hailing from Kosovo and North Macedonia alone. During 2022, around 70,000 Ukrainian refugees found protection in Switzerland. Finally, when new Member States join the EU, Switzerland is obliged to extend its Agreement on the Free Movement of Persons with the EU to these new Members. Hence, since 1 January 2022 Croatians have enjoyed the same rights as other EU citizens.

Cohesion Billions and Focus Regions: How Switzerland Supports Enlargement

Switzerland recognises being a beneficiary of the EU's enlargement policy regarding its stability and development effects and has been willing to support it as a non-Member. In 2006, Switzerland and the EU signed a first Memorandum of Understanding (MoU) on a Swiss contribution to EU enlargement. Switzerland committed to spending CHF 1 billion for the then new EU Member States, on a wide variety of projects related, for instance, to administrative capacity, border security, the environment, infrastructure, the private sector, research, education and health. This programme was extended to Bulgaria, Romania and Croatia (with additional funding). In 2019, Switzerland agreed in principle to a second contribution of CHF 1.3 billion for another 10 years with the same 13 countries. The new MoU recognised 'the close links between Switzerland and the EU', 'the EU's contribution towards safeguarding peace, freedom, stability and prosperity in Europe' along with the country's determination to continue its strong support.

However, the second contribution initially fell prey to the EU-Swiss conflict on the Institutional Framework Agreement that the EU insists on as a prerequisite for continuing and deepening the 'bilateral way' of EU-Swiss relations. After the EU had refused to extend its recognition of equivalence for the Swiss stock exchange in June 2019, the Swiss Parliament made release of the 'cohesion billion' conditional on the EU's 'non-discrimination' of Switzerland. This non-discrimination clause was removed only in September 2021, once the Swiss government had rejected the Institutional Framework Agreement and sought ways to mend relations with the EU. Accordingly, in June 2022, the MoU was finally signed.

This new programme splits the money between cooperating in the areas of cohesion (CHF 1.1 billion) and funding EU Member States heavily affected by migration (CHF 0.2 billion). It also makes professional training a new focus of support. The programme is based on the principle of bilateral project funding, with Switzerland paying into neither the EU's budget nor the national budgets of partner countries. Yet, the 'cohesion billion' benefits only EU Member States. It does not fund projects in any potential candidate countries.

Support for these countries is part of Swiss international development cooperation. Eastern Europe (including both the Western Balkans and the former Soviet Union) has the status of a focus region, the cooperation goals for which are well aligned with the EU accession process's 'modernisation' programme. These goals include democracy, good governance and economic competitiveness. In the Western Balkans, they also orient themselves explicitly towards the EU's accession priorities and support for European integration. The annual budget for cooperation with Eastern Europe has been set at approximately CHF 140 million in recent years and thus similar in size to the prospective annual expenses of the enlargement contribution. Whereas Switzerland provides additional humanitarian aid to Ukraine and the wider region in response to the Russian invasion, it has not changed its current development cooperation programmes. However, the Ukraine programme ends in 2023, offering an opportunity for alignment with the EU's enlargement perspectives.

Recommendations

The EU's decision has formally recognised the Eastern European Association Trio as (potential) candidates for membership. Moreover, reinvigorating the accession process of the Western Balkans countries is a historic mission that promises enormous benefits for European stability and development in the long run, albeit creating massive costs and risks in the short run. Even as a non-Member State, Switzerland is strongly affected by the outcome of this historic mission.

Switzerland should further strengthen its coordination of foreign and development policies with Brussels towards the EU enlargement regions to generate synergies and avoid duplication or tensions. Whereas Switzerland has focused its enlargement contribution to the EU on cooperation with the (not so) new Member States, financial and technical support for the candidate countries of the Western Balkans and Eastern Europe is now of utmost importance. Switzerland should therefore commit to an additional programme specifically designed for candidate countries' needs in the accession process. At the same time, the EU and Switzerland need to make sure that their bilateral conflicts stop blocking this common interest and endeavour.

Frank Schimmelfennig , Ph.D., is Professor of European Politics at ETH Zurich. He is also a member of the Swiss National Research Council, an Associate of the Robert Schuman Centre for Advanced Studies at the European University Institute, and Chairman of the Scientific Board of Institut für Europäische Politik Berlin. His research focuses on the theory and development of European integration. His most recent books on the EU are Ever Looser Union? Differentiated European Integration (Oxford University Press, 2020, with Thomas Winzen) and Integration and Differentiation in the European Union: Theory and Policies (Palgrave, 2022, with Dirk Leuffen and Berthold Rittberger).

The Centre for Comparative and International Studies (CIS) is a joint research centre of political scientists at the ETH Zurich and the University of Zurich, offering a master's programme (MACIS). CIS is a TEPSA member.

Schrödinger's Candidate: Türkiye's Awkward Situation Within the Enlargement Debate

Özgehan Şenyuva and Ali Baydarol

Türkiye stands in a particular and even awkward position regarding debate on the Future of Europe and especially the issue of enlargement. The country has been waiting for membership longer than any other applicant States, with negotiations currently on a de facto hold and any prospects of accession in near future extremely slim. However, Türkiye also remains an important partner and ally for Europe as well as being a member of the Customs Union and holding a critically strategic position regarding irregular migration based on the 2016 European Union (EU)-Türkiye Statement. With the question of EU enlargement towards the Western Balkans and Moldova, Ukraine and Georgia, Türkiye's positions and actions are important for two interconnected reasons. Firstly, Türkiye is very active in these regions and carries great historic, cultural and economic weight. Thus, Türkiye's position in these States' membership aspirations carries certain value. Secondly, Türkiye must calculate and elaborate on the effects of such an enlargement process *vis-à-vis* its own membership bid, notwithstanding that the country's role in the region is seen by some EU Member States as being competitive. Hence, countering Türkiye's potential influence in this context is listed among reasons for the EU to proceed with offering a membership perspective for the Western Balkans States plus Moldova, Ukraine and Georgia. Enlargement must therefore factor in Türkiye's position.

Ö. Şenyuva (✉)
Middle East Technical University, Ankara, Türkiye

Ankara, Türkiye
e-mail: senyuva@metu.edu.tr

A. Baydarol
Sabancı University, Tuzla, Türkiye
e-mail: alibaydarol@sabanciuniv.edu

© The Author(s), under exclusive license to Springer Nature Switzerland AG 2023
M. Kaeding et al. (eds.), *Enlargement and the Future of Europe*,
https://doi.org/10.1007/978-3-031-43234-7_39

Türkiye and the EU: Mutual Mistrust and Lack of Progress

In a way, EU-Türkiye relations are a relationship of mutual insincerity and mistrust. On the one hand, the EU has for many years tended to keep membership as a possibility, on condition that Türkiye meets the Copenhagen Criteria. On the other hand, Türkiye pretended to remain committed to its membership goal and the fundamentals of liberal democracy. However, in reality liberal intergovernmentalism and bargaining appears best to explain Türkiye's membership process. In the last two decades it has been dominated by identity and power politics based on interests rather than remaining a legal and technical issue based on values. Worsened by Türkiye's democratic backslide and increased failings in rights and liberties, the whole membership process has been overshadowed, thus allowing Türkiye's European and liberal credentials to became highly questionable. Accordingly, Türkiye is no longer being discussed as a potential Member in the next potential enlargement wave. Even worse, due to increased tensions with EU Members such as Greece and Cyprus, even Türkiye's position as a reliable ally is being doubted. Some politicians in EU Member States aim to make political gains both at domestic and international levels through 'Türkiye bashing' in attempts to profit from weakening relations between Türkiye and the other European states. Hence, one must consider this climate when analysing Türkiye's potential position and activity *vis-à-vis* Union enlargement towards the West Balkans as well as Moldova, Georgia and Ukraine. The EU should communicate with Ankara and keep them included as much as possible, to underline the fact this is not another attempt in further isolating and excluding Türkiye. In 2024, the big bang enlargement of 2004 will be in its 20th year. It is certainly hard to say that Turkish public opinion and the politicians have yet to recover from the sense of exclusion and being subjected to double standards. On the contrary, with the developments that followed, such as suspension of negotiation chapters by certain EU Member States and increased anti-Turkish rhetoric, Türkiye's mistrust only worsened. For instance, while 68% of respondents in Türkiye favoured or strongly favoured EU membership in 2005, support fell to 54% in 2022. Nevertheless, this does not automatically lead to EU rejectionism. When asked whether another model of relations with the EU other than membership should be established or not in 2022, a sound majority of the respondents (68%) rejected any other form of relationship besides membership. However, any realistic belief in Türkiye's EU membership potential is now almost non-existent: in 2022, 61% of respondents think that Türkiye will never become a full Member of the EU.

On the positive side, though, EU-Türkiye relationsremain solid in some issue areas. In particular, economic relations have advanced over the years, which has created a mutual dependency, with Türkiye being the more dependent side. Hence, even without the possibility of enlargement, the EU still has a critical role in Türkiye's economic well-being.

Türkiye in the Region: An Ally to Cooperate or a Rival to Compete?

The Russia's War in Ukraine has shown that having positive relations with Türkiye could help the EU to cooperate with the Eastern Neighbourhood and Western Balkan countries more efficiently for three reasons.

Firstly, the war has deepened the EU's energy crisis. With natural gas imports from Russia having been reduced, the EU has leaned towards alternative sources, one of them being Azerbaijani gas. This energy transfer is made through the Trans-Anatolian Gas Pipeline that bridges Azerbaijan and the EU through Türkiye. Secondly, the war closed many Northern trade routes, leaving those through Türkiye as alternatives. Hence, Türkiye now also plays a critical role for the EU's supply chain. Thirdly, the war has made Türkiye the region's current grain supplier.

Thus, it can be argued that improving relations with Türkiye through a feasible agenda would be to the EU's benefit. The two parties can work on updating the EU-Türkiye Customs Union and visa liberalisation, even though boosting democracy reforms and inclusion of Türkiye in the EU's enlargement agenda are not viable for now.

Lessons from Türkiye in the Region

In the 2000s, the EU supported Türkiye's mass privatisation programme. However, as with those in the Western Balkans, these privatisations have led to the formation of clientelist networks. Hence, instead of utilising a swift, united approach, the EU may employ a gradual approach with specific institutional priorities (such as the rule of law). After all, without the institutions that ensure transparency in public auctions and tenders, economic reforms might well-truncate the democratic qualities of regimes. Pressuring for swift structural reforms may produce undesirable consequences. For instance, the EU's privatisation pressures on Serbia led to the sale of large state-owned enterprises in an environment where there were no institutions to ensure meritocracy-based privatisation. The result, not unlike Türkiye, was the establishment of clientelist networks between the incumbents and pro-government business actors. The argument extends to the Western Balkans, including North Macedonia, Bosnia and Herzegovina. The EU should also bear in mind the negative impact of prolonging the membership process and making it an ever-moving target, which may create candidacy fatigue, as it is the case in Türkiye. Once a country such as Moldova, for instance, enters the membership path, it needs to remain active with certain achievements realised and thresholds passed. Otherwise, the pro-EU actors within the current political divide in the country will slowly lose power and credibility. This is exactly the case for Türkiye, where owning the EU membership goal became highly risky and difficult as a result of constant distancing of eventual membership, due especially to the interest-driven actions of some Member States.

Currently, candidates from the West Balkans and Moldova, Ukraine and Georgia are still far from functioning as stable liberal democracies. This situation is one of the reasons why the EU will face serious challenges for further integration in the future. Employing a gradual approach with specific institutional priorities would enable the EU to transform and move these countries in the desired direction. Furthermore, as they gradually improve their democracy and market-economy qualities, the EU can reward these achievements with the opening/closing of acquis chapters and financial support. More promising membership prospects would ensure that candidate countries do not need to search for alternative allies to the EU.

Recommendations

The EU and its Member States should be mindful that Türkiye is neither a rival nor a competitor in the region. It is an accession country, with enduring sizeable public support for full membership. There are two steps the EU can take: firstly, it can support any future democratic steps in Türkiye and put relations back onto a technical and legal footing based on values; and secondly, the EU can deepen functioning cooperation and act as an ally on hard issues. Turkish public opinion would be supportive of any concrete and transparent development in Türkiye-EU relations and it would help to restore trust. Upgrading of the Customs Union offers a huge potential, as it would also enable Türkiye to benefit from EU enlargement in the regions where it holds economic interests. Finally, the EU should draw lessons from Türkiye's membership process and its failures: the enlargement policy should have credibility and transparency in the eyes of new candidates and they should know that their bid will not be sacrificed for domestic and national political calculations.

Özgehan Şenyuva, Ph.D., is affiliated with the Centre for European Studies at Middle East Technical University, Ankara. He gained his PhD from the University of Siena and works extensively on public opinion, European Union and the politics of football. He is also a well-known researcher and speaker on Youth Work and Learning Mobility.

Centre for European Studies CES-METU is a multi-disciplinary research centre under the Faculty of Economic and Administrative Sciences at the Middle East Technical University. It brings together researchers working on different aspects of European issues. CES-METU has been the pioneer and leading institution in European Studies in Türkiye and other pan European research projects.

Ali Baydarol is a PhD candidate in political science and a graduate teaching assistant at the Faculty of Arts and Social Sciences, Sabancı University. He is also a research assistant in the TÜBİTAK 1001 project entitled 'The Role of Elite Sociology in Understanding the Policy Making Process of Türkiye-European Union Relations' at Bahçeşehir University. He gained his MA from Radboud University and conducts research on the issues of comparative political economy and the European Union. He also worked as the research assistant at the Istanbul Policy Centre, which is a global policy research institution that specialises in key social and political issues ranging from democratisation to climate change, transatlantic relations to conflict resolution and mediation.

Founded in 1994 by the Sabancı Group, Sabancı University is a research-oriented institution located in Istanbul, Türkiye. Under the Faculty of Arts and Social Sciences, the university is dedicated to fostering interdisciplinary research and collaboration among leading social scientists across various fields. Sabancı University continues to respond to the ever-increasing needs of the society with its efforts in education, teaching as well as research and maintains direct involvement with society to understand current and future needs.

On the Outside Looking in: The United Kingdom After Brexit

Brendan Donnelly

During nearly 50 years of the United Kingdom's (UK) membership in the European Union (EU), there were various cross-currents to British debate on EU enlargement. The British Foreign Office wished to promote enlargement for Eastern and Central Europe as a way of securing the prosperity and democracy of which it had been deprived during the Cold War. The British political class more broadly wished to promote enlargement in the hope that the Union's geographic widening would impede its political deepening. British public opinion for its part was either indifferent or apprehensive about the Union's enlargement. Even after Brexit, traces of these conflicting attitudes surface in the (albeit very limited) continuing political discussion within the UK on this issue.

Between 2016 and 2022 the topic of EU enlargement disappeared almost entirely from British political discourse. Shortly after the Brexit referendum, the then British Foreign Secretary Boris Johnson was rash enough to remark publicly that the UK supported Turkish accession to the EU. The widespread ridicule which greeted this utterance from one of Brexit's main architects for many years thereafter deterred Johnson and his successors from further public pronouncements upon future EU enlargement. The Ukraine war though has rekindled UK discussion and speculation about the future security architecture of Europe and the British role therein. The EU's future boundaries and activities inevitably form part of this debate.

After the Ukraine War

As with so much of the European debate in the UK, British reactions to the Ukraine war have often been crude and opportunistic. Boris Johnson, for instance, absurdly compared Ukrainian resistance to the Russian invasion with Brexit, while there has

---

B. Donnelly (✉)
The Federal Trust, London, UK
e-mail: brendan.donnelly@fedtrust.co.uk

been criticism of German 'pacifism' from others who in only slightly different circumstances would have warned loudly against German militarism. However, behind the posturing certain preferences are emerging among the British political elite, which may be shared, at least in part, by future British governments.

During British EU membership, there were many in the UK, even among supporters of British membership, who believed that the Union was an excessively introverted organisation, an introversion supposedly shown by its disinclination to accept new Members such as Türkiye and Ukraine. This view has not disappeared and most British public and political opinion would be sympathetic to rapid Ukrainian membership of the EU. This generalised sympathy would though be subject to two important caveats, which once again reflect traditional British views about EU enlargement.

The Right Kind of Enlargement

The first is that EU enlargement to Ukraine (or any other country in the Western Balkans) should not be associated with a deepening of the EU, particularly not with any deepening of its military responsibilities. For any foreseeable British government, the military security of a non-Russian Europe will be a matter for NATO exclusively. Greater military integration through the EU would in the traditional British view at best be a duplication of existing NATO activity and might well be ultimately harmful to the Alliance's coherence. Seen from London, there are various EU member states that should significantly increase their contribution to Europe's physical defence, not least Germany. However, this enhanced contribution is above all a NATO-related responsibility. The EU in this context is at best an irrelevance and more probably a distraction.

The second caveat is reflected in reports from May 2022 that Boris Johnson had presented to the Ukrainian President a proposal for a 'European Commonwealth', in which Ukraine, Turkey and possibly the Baltic States might participate. It is an article of faith for many British Eurosceptics that the EU is and will always be on the brink of collapse and irreparable division. Many of these British Eurosceptics regard the varying reactions of different EU Member States to the Ukraine war as reinforcing this analysis. Boris Johnson's proposal for a European Commonwealth (of which little more has since been heard) derives from this analysis. More generally, so long as the UK remains outside the EU, it will always see the question of EU enlargement through the prism of its own perceived national interest. Within the present Conservative government in London, there are certainly those who see disruption of the EU as being in the UK's national interest. Time will tell whether this view is held by a majority within this present Conservative government and how far will future governments seek to imitate their Conservative predecessors. Settlement of the controversy relating to the Northern Ireland Protocol by the new Prime Minister, Rishi Sunak, is seen by some as presaging a more cordial tone to EU/UK relations for the coming months. A constructive role for the UK in developing a

European Political Community is a possible future expression of this enhanced cordiality.

The current British government is aware that its capacity to influence the EU's internal debates is very limited. It cannot in any meaningful way affect the complex debate about the balance to be struck between encouragement for success and punishment for failure regarding necessary reforms in candidate countries. Nor can it exercise its traditional restraining role on those Member States who regard institutional deepening of the EU as a necessary precondition for the Union's further enlargement. Ironically, there are many among the most radical Eurosceptics in the UK who would welcome further deepening of the EU's integrative structures, reasoning that it would make re-entry into the Union more unattractive to the British electorate. History suggests that such speculative calculations are likely to be as wildly incorrect as presciently accurate.

Recommendations

Brexit is a self-reinforcing tragedy for the United Kingdom, a fact which makes recommendations for its improvement particularly difficult. The British government would though be well advised to: (a) abandon all thoughts that it can construct within Europe an alternative pole of attraction to the EU; (b) accept that the EU can and perhaps will need to deepen its responsibility for its own physical defence; (c) cease using its own creditable contribution to the defence of Ukraine as a pretext for denigrating its European partners; and (d) stress to the British public that the Ukraine war demonstrates a need for European unity, to which the UK wishes to contribute. Within the context of current European debate in the UK, these preceding recommendations are radical indeed.

Brendan Donnelly has been Director of the research institute The Federal Trust in London since January 2003. He was a Conservative MEP from 1994 until 1999 and had previously worked for the British Foreign Office, the European Commission and the Conservative Group in the European Parliament.

The Federal Trust is a think tank that studies the interactions between regional, national, European and global levels of government. Since its founding in 1945, it has devoted itself particularly to the study of federalism and federal systems. It has always had a specific interest in the European Union and Britain's relationship with it.

EU Enlargement Considering New Realities: The Ukrainian Direction

Yuriy Yakymenko and Mykhailo Pashkov

In 2022 the European Union (EU) faced new circumstances and challenges that substantially changed its philosophy, principles and motives for further enlargement. This was caused by interrelated processes, namely the unprecedentedly severe clash between the collective West and an aggressive Russian Federation versus increasing global confrontation between the democratic civilised world and a camp of totalitarian states. Hence, the process of EU enlargement as a constituent part of its foreign policy will be increasingly shaped by political and security factors, which are now not just decisive for Europe, but the whole world. Ukraine is very much the focus of confrontation amongst global powers in Europe now, which determines the exclusiveness and importance of its integration into the EU.

The Cost of European Integration for Ukraine

Brussels is strategically interested in both resistance to Russian expansion into Ukraine as well as maintenance of inter-ethnic peace and institutional stability in the conflict-ridden Balkan region. Integrated expansion as practised by Brussels is certainly a tested and most efficient enlargement tool in the area of stability for Europe. However, it should be accepted that the weight and cost of European integration for Balkan citizens versus Ukrainians are different, to put it mildly. With Ukraine defending the EU's eastern flank against the Kremlin's armed aggression on a 1000 km long front, it is no exaggeration to suggest that the future of Europe depends on the Ukrainian army.

During Russia's unprovoked invasion, one of the deadliest in Europe since the Second World War, Ukraine has sustained colossal human, financial and economic losses. The aggressor practices missile terror against the civilian population

Y. Yakymenko · M. Pashkov (✉)
Razumkov Centre, Kyiv, Ukraine
e-mail: pashkov@razumkov.org.ua

intentionally ruins Ukraine's housing, utilities, energy infrastructure, educational establishments and historic monuments. It pursues a policy of genocide against the Ukrainian nation, ultimately dedicated to its physical elimination.

Notably, this long all-out war has firstly demonstrated the readiness of Ukrainians to defend the sovereignty of their country and its development along the European path. Secondly, it has intensified the bilateral processes of European integration and changed the quality of Brussels' policy regarding Ukraine. Thirdly, it has contributed to the unity and cohesion of the Ukrainian nation, enhanced public support for its movement to the EU and the processes of pro-European self-identification for citizens.

This is evidenced by the results of sociological surveys held by the Razumkov Centre. Public support for Ukraine's accession to the EU is steadily gaining momentum. For instance, in March 2021, 59% of citizens believed that Ukraine should join the EU, but by October 2022, this share had increased to 79% (poll conducted by the Razumkov Centre Sociological Service) between 22 September and 1 October 2022 in all regions of Ukraine, except for the Crimea and occupied territories of Donetsk, Luhansk and Kherson regions. In the Zaporizhia, Mykolaiv and Kharkiv regions, results reflected only those territories which are controlled by the Ukrainian government and free from hostilities. Meanwhile, in 2022 public sentiments were clearly dominated by the processes of pro-European self-identification. While in previous years citizens were doubtful about their European identity, by October 2022, 63% not only reported feeling like Europeans, but also felt affiliation with the culture and traditions of the European community.

Ukraine's acquisition of candidate status for EU membership certainly became a symbolic milestone event that gave an impetus to domestic socio-economic reforms, morally and psychologically encouraged Ukrainians, fighting for their country's European future.

Current Tasks for Europe

Under conditions of war, Ukraine continues pro-European reforms in different areas, from the protection of human rights, social policy, energy and transport to digitalisation, public procurements and environmental protection. Progress in 24 priority areas is tracked in the government's online monitoring system 'Pulse of the Agreement'. Kyiv is deepening sectoral cooperation with Brussels, implementing provisions of the Agreement of Association and following the European Commission's recommendations. Currently, the most important domains that require additional efforts include effective operation in the system of anti-corruption bodies and completion of judicial reform. In general, Ukraine needs three key conditions in implementing pro-European reforms: political will; the large-scale support of citizens and consistent assistance from the European Community.

Although the 24th Ukraine-EU Summit in February 2023 did not fully meet some of the Ukrainian authorities' inflated hopes, its results were nevertheless important. These included providing all-round assistance to Kyiv in resisting Russian aggression, implementing reforms, accelerating integration into the EU markets and determining further guidelines for European integration (interim assessment in the spring of 2023 and a final report within the framework of the enlargement package by autumn).

In 2023, while in war, the Ukrainian government a) adopted a number of basic laws and implemented reforms as part of the European Commission's "homework"; b) conducted an extensive self-audit of the national legislation's compliance with EU norms; c) in recent months alone, adopted a number of important pro-European acts in various areas. All in all, this gives grounds to expect a positive report from the European Commission and a green light from the European Council to start the EU membership talks.

KYIV-Brussels: Strategic and Tactical Priorities

It is possible to single out a few key areas on which to focus:

1. this includes introduction of the 'European lend-lease', namely the prompt provision of comprehensive military assistance to Ukraine, to include: a regular supply of the necessary weapon; systemic financial support from the European Peace Fund; the establishment of joint defence industry enterprises and the expansion of training programmes for the Ukrainian military.
2. there is a need to implement the plan for Ukraine's integration into European markets through: further liberalisation of trade cooperation; introduction of joint production, industrial, infrastructural projects, intensification of the EU investment policy; as well as the efficient employment of streamlined 'visa-free procedures' in energy, trade, customs and transport.
3. the 'visa-free industry' should be subject to an accelerated launch by way of an agreement on Conformity Assessment and Acceptance of industrial products (ACAA).
4. Ukraine needs to be integrated into the 'Digital Europe' programme.
5. target programmes for the Ukrainian economy's recovery will need to be implemented, covering: ruined infrastructure, housing and utilities; the social and cultural sector; assistance to small and medium businesses (latest calculations indicate that the EU package of credit assistance totalling EUR 18 billion for 2023 will only partially resolve the problem of social budget expenditures in Ukraine).
6. Priorities of the EU-Ukraine agenda include implementing Ukraine's Peace Formula, concluding agreements on the provision of security guarantees to Kyiv under the G7 Joint Declaration of Support for Ukraine, and finding a legal formula for compensating Ukraine for its losses from the war at the expense of the aggressor's frozen funds.
7. most importantly, a joint common position from EU Member States should be established regarding the beginning of negotiations on Ukraine's accession.

EU Enlargement Policy: Specificities and Prospects

At the end of 2022, new prospective EU Members appeared. Bosnia and Herzegovina obtained candidate status, while Kosovo submitted its application for admission. This situation, on the one hand, complicates the process of further enlargement, particularly by adding scepticism to the opponents of enlargement in the countries of 'old Europe'. On the other hand, it actualises the need for internal reforms within the EU. In this respect, in the authors' opinion, the following steps seem reasonable:

Firstly, the European Council should develop and adopt a new strategic concept of EU enlargement that will set out the principles, bases, ways and prospects of admission for new countries to the EU. This should take into account the present-day realities and threats, as well as the present situation's dynamics in Europe.

Secondly, the EU and its Member States' leadership should accumulate political will for updating the EU's basic documents to part with 'the curse of consensus' and shift to decision-making by a qualified majority. The benefits are evident, given the regular abuse of veto by countries such as Hungary.

Thirdly, the EU 'Strategic Compass' should be updated with an account of the current situation and view further enlargement of the EU as a key foreign policy priority, the tool for countering threats and challenges on the European continent.

Fourthly, the enlargement policy should be released from the 'one basket' traditional package approach. Candidate countries are at different stages of their movement to the EU and in different 'weight classes', with regard inter alia to the 'security relevance', current threats and challenges. Specifically, for Ukraine accession to the EU presents a key tool for the defence of freedom and national statehood.

Fifthly, official institute of curator countries, assisting with European integration of the candidates for admission, should be introduced.

Sixthly and lastly, present-day realities prompt the idea of further EU enlargement as a tool for countering internal and external challenges as well as threats, in particular expansion of the aggressive 'Russian world' into Europe. In this respect, a unified political will and resolve from Brussels' eastern, primarily Ukrainian, policy acquires particular significance.

Co-funded by
the European Union

The European Commission's support for production of this publication does not constitute an endorsement of the contents, which reflect the views only of the authors. Moreover, the Commission cannot be held responsible for any use which may be made of the information contained herein.

Yuriy Yakymenko, Ph.D., is the President of the Razumkov Centre (Kyiv, Ukraine). Before joining the Razumkov Centre, he worked at the Administration of the President of Ukraine as the political analyst from 1995 to 2002, Head of Division for liaison with political parties and public organisation, Deputy Head of the Main Department of Political Analysis and Forecast. He studied political science at Kyiv Taras Shevchenko University, obtained MA degree in Political Theory at The University of Manchester (1994) and holds a Ph.D. in Political Science.

Mykhailo Pashkov, Ph.D., has been Co-director of Foreign Relations and International Security Programmes at the Razumkov Centre since 2010. He graduated from the Smolensk Pedagogical Institute (1979); Moscow Youth Institute, Faculty of Journalism (1986); Kyiv Institute of Political Science and Social Management (1991). He is a political scientist with vast experience and particular expertise on Russia-Ukraine politics, NATO, European and Euro-Atlantic integration. Before joining the Razumkov Centre he worked at the National Academy of Sciences of Ukraine and served as diplomat at the Embassy of Ukraine in the Russian Federation and as chief consultant at the Analytical Service of the National Security and Defence Council.

The Razumkov Centre is a non-governmental think tank founded in 1994, uniting experts in the fields of: economy, energy, law, political sciences, international relations, military security, land relations, sociology, history and philosophy. The Centre is also a member of TEPSA.

GPSR Compliance

The European Union's (EU) General Product Safety Regulation (GPSR) is a set of rules that requires consumer products to be safe and our obligations to ensure this.

If you have any concerns about our products, you can contact us on

ProductSafety@springernature.com

In case Publisher is established outside the EU, the EU authorized representative is:

Springer Nature Customer Service Center GmbH
Europaplatz 3
69115 Heidelberg, Germany

www.ingramcontent.com/pod-product-compliance
Lightning Source LLC
LaVergne TN
LVHW010341260326
834688LV00036B/818

GPSR Compliance

The European Union's (EU) General Product Safety Regulation (GPSR) is a set of rules that requires consumer products to be safe and our obligations to ensure this.

If you have any concerns about our products, you can contact us on

ProductSafety@springernature.com

In case Publisher is established outside the EU, the EU authorized representative is:

Springer Nature Customer Service Center GmbH
Europaplatz 3
69115 Heidelberg, Germany